HEATHER

A Married Woman's Haunted Life

Heather M. Alfred

Heather M. Alfred

FIRST EDITION

Date Started: July 8, 2008

Completed: May 06, 2019

HEATHER First Edition.

For information, use the following address:

Heather M. Alfred 330 Harper Street Sarepta, La. 71071

Publisher

James M. Murphy

A book dedicated to my husband of 31 years
And my 4 children, 3 Grandchildren and my Dad

CONTENTS

Introduction

N o writing experience means certain failure on my first attempt. I will take that chance. This book is too important for me to fail. I write knowing you will not believe me but I continue to write. Let your heart guide you and please overlook my poor English. I am with average southern high school education. I am religious, but this book is not about religion. However, related to religion and the belief in a higher power I have some thoughts. These may set the stage for what I am here to tell you. If you endorse these thoughts I present, perhaps you can believe the rest of this book.

Do not let people change your destiny about where you want to go in life. Do not get off course and allow God to lead you down life's path. Walk and talk with God through prayer and He will provide the answer. I may have average intelligence but smart enough to know to do these important things and things I should not do.

Do not listen to the words of man when they contradict God. Man can be the deceiver as the devil is. If you do not believe in God, devil, or the after life, you must read this book. Perhaps I can change your mind with knowledge no one has ever provided you.

When God speaks to you, you must obey him no matter what. I feel like God is guiding me to write this book to show His glory. If I did not write this book to let you learn how deceitful the devil can be, he would win the battle I been fighting for over 11 years. Today I still fight him.

I feel others fight the same kind of demon spirits. I am not sure what caused my demons to show themselves. I can tell you how I try to get rid of them when they come back. They will return to test you at times. I maintain God lets the devil test our faith in God himself. I might be wrong but this is what I firmly believe.

As you read my story, you may or may not believe it. I am writing this book to the best of my memory and truthfully. I have witnesses to back up my stories as well. I know people will judge or ridicule me. However, when God speaks we must listen.

I hope and pray that my story will help others that are going through the same battles. There is hope and you can win. You must keep the word of God in your heart, mind, and mouth daily. God is the only one that can fight this form of battle. Through Him you can, defeat the devil and take authority, back over your home and life.

Once you learn to take authority over your home and life will become easier to fight the enemy. You must stay in God's word at all times. I found if you backslide from God that He will let the devil attack you again. They will come back to haunt you if you keep the door open.

I have learned from experience that you want to keep the door closed from demonic attacks. If not, each time they will become stronger. It is very important to stay in God's living word daily. The demonic spirits will attack the weak and the strong. Weak minded will not win the battles of demons but a strong mind can send them back to hell.

Matthew 12:45 Then goeth he, and taketh with himself seven other spirits more wicked than himself, and they enter in and dwell there: and the last state of the man is worse than the first. Even so shall it be also unto this wicked generation.

The story I am writing intends to show you how to overcome demon spirits when they attack you. One must be prepared to fight a battle that only the power of God's words can win. This is not a book about the Bible but a book that contains references to the Bible when they relate to the story I am telling.

HEATHER

Chapter

1

Confused Mind

H i, I am Heather Murphy Alfred. I am just an average wife with a husband of 30 years. I graduated with a high school diploma and no college education. My family lives in a small town in a small mobile home. We are ordinary people living ordinary lives. As working parents with four children, we need to give them a lot of attention and focus.

When you live a chaotic life, it can be confusing to think which way in life you wish to go. I sometimes thought I should have gone to college or done something more with my life. I hated school, so I knew further education would not be for me. My husband and I both work retail and make a small joint income. Nevertheless, I always said money does not buy love or happiness. Not having it creates problems.

I live a simple life and do not understand why things seem to happen to me. I try to do the right things but sometimes they turn out to be the wrong ones. I would like to know why this happens. I toss it up to a case of bad luck. Alternatively, I being of Murphy bloodline may play a role. Maybe Murphy's Law "anything that can go wrong will go wrong" is at work.

I have learned over the years we do not have bad luck we just make bad decisions in life. We teach what is right and wrong early in life. Those choices guide our destiny. Making life choices is the biggest decision one makes for their self. Only you can decide your destiny in life influenced by circumstances beyond your control.

When I was young, I had a hard time making decisions and asked others for their opinion. Then I would decide which way to go. I was always the follower and not the leader. That was probably not the right thing to do. The older I get, the more I do not want others to give their opinion. I sometimes feel like a child still when I have to ask for permission to do something. Maybe that set up some hostility towards life.

I got married at the early age of 15. My husband was 22. He was always and still is the head of household and makes the primary decisions. We do not have a lot but we make do with what we do have. However, I always said money could not buy love. I had rather have love over money. He takes care of the bills, taxes, and things like that. I never had the desire to know how to do that. I, being young, knew nothing about these things. I think this is when I started to not having the experience of independence.

Married at a young age, I knew nothing about what I wanted in life. This was too young to get married. Before making my decisions, I would always ask my husband what to do first. Being so young, I did not mind asking him because I needed his advice. He was 7 years older than I was then. However, when I got older, the outcome of his decisions changed in my mind. This now causes conflicts when we disagree on things.

The older I get, the more I wish to carry out my own decisions and dream of independence. However, being married you know that will never happen. Not saying being married is bad, just suggesting it has limits to what you can or cannot do without having to ask your spouse. You must learn to compromise for both of you to be happy. When that happens, it delights everyone. Nevertheless, sometimes you lose your happiness in the mix to make others happy. That can cause problems. For example, confrontations you do not want to face by talking about a controversial subject.

Because I wed at a young age, at first, life was hard. I married to get out of my home. I am Dad's only child. Dad worked all the time and we would always travel a lot too. I had a step-mom I did not get along with at the time. My real Mom had four other children and another husband. My stepfather was a good person, and I loved him dearly. I was living from house to house most of my childhood existence. I would stay at Mom's house and tire of living there. Then go to my Dad's or Grandmother's and so back to Moms. I spent my childhood existence living out of a suitcase.

Living out of that suitcase my childhood development was difficult. I changed school several times a year that made it hard to find friends. I was never a social person and did not have many friends. I was a quiet girl and stayed to myself mostly in school. I hated school because of my anxiety. I did not have a stable home life to teach me right or wrong decisions. Moving from one place to another caused confusion in my young head.

Maybe this is why I was a confused and unsure person because I never had stability in my life. All I wanted in life was to be happy and have a family that was happy together. The family I had when I was little was not a happy home. My parents divorced when I was like five. I remember sitting in the courtroom telling them who I wanted to live with. I said my Mom however; the court sent me to my Dad's home.

Living with my Dad was probably the best decision the judge ruled for me. Being that little I would have never known what was best. All I remember is I loved both my parents and unable to understand why they divorced. It was until I got older I realized why they did. It was from drug habits that my Mom had. The same reason the judge chose my Dad that day in court. To this day, I understand that drugs can ruin a family. As I said, choices in life guide your destiny.

Unfortunately, my Mom did not want me because of her drug issues at that time. I loved my Mom, but she had many issues. I recall a night when I was about four or five-year-old running down a street. One of her old boyfriends was chasing us with an ax. I was so scared and crying. My grandmother was near us in her car. She picked us up to take us to her house. I have never forgotten that night. After that, I always had dreams from then on that someone was chasing me.

Later in life when I got older, I had a good relationship with my Mom. I know she had her faults, but we all do. I never had a bad relationship with her. We always got along just fine. I had three other sisters and one brother that she and my stepfather raised. He unfortunately died September 1995 and then her in September 1996. I recall how bad she treated them. Wherefore, my stepfather treated them good. However, she treated me different. I felt like her treating me different caused a broken wedge between my sibling and me. We all were never real close.

I lived with my Dad and he worked all the time. I was a little girl trying to find stability in a home that did not have my Mom or Dad in it. Always felt like I was looking for something. I was, looking for a happy home. Makes me wonder now is this why I have a confused mind. I had a family, but they did not have much to do with me most of my life. We also lived far apart. I lived in Louisiana while they lived in Florida at that time.

Not saying I had bad parents, we all make mistakes and bad choices in life. I love both parents the same. Although one worked all the time and other one had drug issues, they were still my parents. Neither was really in my life the way I needed them to be. I needed both. I believe we all need both parents in our lives. However, even sometimes with both parents one can turn down the wrong path. Therefore, I am not saying having parents together or not makes you perfect. Because it is the choices, we make in life that guides your path forward.

Proverbs 3:6 In all thy ways acknowledge him, and he shall direct thy paths.

My husband and I both come from broken homes. When we married, we said we would work through anything that came our way. For better or worse until death, do we part? Wedding vows are important to us in our marriage. People said we would never make it. We have been through many things in past 30 years too.

Parents should try to stay together for sake of your kids when you have problems in a relationship if possible. They are the ones that would get hurt in process. No child wants to come from a broken home. These are experienced words of a broken home child. Nevertheless, I understand certain situations it may be better for the child and not stay together. Unfortunately, my parents used to get into many arguments, which was not healthy to see. We as children need to feel love and happiness, not to tolerate anger and hate.

I believe that getting married at an early age seemed to be the logical thing to do in my situation. By no means has our marriage been a bed of roses. No marriage is perfect, and neither is anyone's life. God created us to fail and make mistakes. We must have faith that He will get us through our mistakes in life. Even in a marriage, we all make mistakes. We can say and do hurtful things to one another. That is when we forgive one another and work it out. The devil loves to cause arguments and pain of our loved ones. He does not want us to be happy humans. As I said, no marriage is perfect.

My primary confrontation is not with my husband. Somehow, in the past, we invited guest that will not leave. Maybe it was done out of anger we all show each other at times. Perhaps invited thru books, magazines, or movies as some religions believe. Perhaps it was via items previously owned by deceased relatives. Whatever it was that invited them to come, I now want them to leave. I never want them in my home again. Get out! I know this sounds harsh, so let me explain my reasons by telling you my story.

First, I need to tell you some of my opinions about life and the after life. Then we will journey together and discuss what has been my married woman's haunted life.

Past several years I experienced life and death situations. Best part of my life was having my four children being born even though I had C-sections with them. God did not create for this body to have children naturally. We planned for the first two children and the last two were surprises by God again. I know how precious life can be when you see your newborn child come into the crazy world we live.

The next best part of life is having my three grandsons come into the world. I saw the first one come into the world and other two I did not see them born. Those boys make life great. These little boys melt my heart. Children are the circle of life and God's gifts.

I have seen loved one's get sick and die as well. I said my goodbyes to Grandma Murphy (Dad's mother) in a hospital with kidney failure. My Nanny was in a nursing home last time I saw her. She died from a stroke because of complications from diabetes. My Stepfather lost the battle to lung cancer. Year after he died my Mother died due to a blood clot in the lungs. There have been many more to mention that I have lost to death.

When my husband's grandpa passed away, we got to the hospital right after he had took last breathe of life in his sleep. When we went into his room, he was at peace. I will never forget being in the hospital room when my husband's grandma passed away. That was the first time I ever saw someone take her last breath of life. She left this world peacefully as well in her sleep.

Life and death are miracle wonders of God. He can give us life and then take it. I know we wonder how God can let things happen but He is out to test of our faith in him. I believe demonic spirits test us to see if we are strong or weak minded.

2 Corinthians 2:11 Lest Satan should get an advantage of us: for we are not ignorant of his devices.

The spiritual forces can confuse your mind too. You must know when a spirit is good or bad. I have experienced both types of spirits. This is probably why I was confused over what was happening years ago. I was like most none believers thinking things like this cannot happen and be truly real. Not sure even what started the attack or where they came from. What I know is I wanted no part of this but they wanted a part of my family and me.

Chapter

2

Evil Spirits & Possessions Exist

E veryone wonders why were put on this earth. With four children, you think you are here because of them. Parents say their children are "God Sent" if the children are "good". Then, you wonder, when the children are "bad", if he sent them to torture you. I accept having children might be the reason I am here, but I wonder about other possibilities.

Maybe God had another plan to add to my already busy life, for me to write a book about my family and our strange experiences within our home. I know many Christians and non-Christians do not believe in evil spirits and possessions. However, I know they do exist. The bible talks about them. Why believe in what the Bible says?

2 Timothy 3:16 All scripture is given by inspiration of God, and is profitable for doctrine, for reproof, for correction, for instruction in righteousness:

The Bible talks about evil spirits and not be deceived by Satan and his angels. There have been many accounts of possessions as well. If you read the Bible, you will see the truth of what I am saying in my true story is real. I am here to tell you that the Bible's words are true. I personally experienced the evil spirits and possessions. I was possessed with a demon and was unaware of it until July 7, 2008. That day my family's life changed forever.

There are many nonbelievers and few believers in evil spirits. I know you are thinking this cannot happen, but my family experienced evil spirits. I would not have believed either if I had not personally had the experience. We suffered for many days with these spirits living in our home. Even to this day, we still experience things from time to time. It has been scary for my family and me. Keep in mind they do come back at times for a faith test.

I was never a believer myself about demons or paranormal activity. However, after this experience I am definitely a believer now. I have had many unexplained things happen to me in the past 11 years of my life. No one would believe all this until the experienced it. This book is to help give an insight of what the spirit world is like. Demons can come in, disrupt a family, and tear them apart. Fortunately, for my family we overcome these demons together and still here to this day. Demons can shake us but not break us.

Matthew 12:43 When the unclean spirit is gone out of a man, he walketh through dry places, seeking rest, and findeth none.

Now I want to give you all a little insight of what we experienced while going through all this. The next thing I will mention will sound unbelievable. Nevertheless, if you were not interested in what I have to say you would not be reading all this now. I hope this book will catch your interest and give you understanding that demons do exist in this world. The things I have seen, felt, and heard would blow your mind as it did mine.

I have seen things move such as canisters, coke can, vegetable cans, chairs, and cabinet and oven doors open. Seen things thrown around my house such as CDs, pictures, can goods, TV remote, toothbrush, and pacifiers. Even my youngest son thrown across the room and my oldest caught him. I have heard baby cries; birds flying, knocks, footsteps and even my Nanny call my name. My hair pulled, blankets pulled off me, scratched, and spit on. I have felt and heard birds flying through my house but never seen them. The baby angels that my oldest son said he has seen I could feel them hold my hands. I felt my Nanny hold me after I heard she said my name. This all sounds unbelievable until I lived it.

The Bible talks about when demon spirits come back they come back with seven stronger spirits than the first.

Therefore, it is important to put on whole armor of God when cleansing your home. Spirits will hide from you. The only way I could find them was through the Holy Spirit guiding me and helping me pray them out of my home.

Matthew 12:44 Then he saith, I will return into my house from whence I came out: and when he is come, he findeth it empty, swept, and garnished.

The Holy Spirit was the only way I could fight these demons out of my house. I prayed through my house in the name of Jesus and rebuking the demons out. At this time, I had no clue how to do this but the Holy Spirit came over me and helped me fight the battle that it would not win. I also opened my Bible and read anything in red to scare them away. I was so scared during that time I knew the Bible was my only hope to get rid of them.

I am sure that you reading this and thinking she is a crazy woman. May be a little crazy but not mental. Raised in church all my life, I always knew that God was real. I was a member of several denomination churches, which preached about different things. Some churches believe in demon spirits and some do not. Baptized in four different churches, not sure how I was possessed but I was. I lived a real life horror movie.

The day I got possessed was a very scary time in my life. I did not understand what was happening to me. I had no control over it and could remember everything that was happening. I become mean and aggressive to anyone that came around me. I hurt no one per se but I scared many loved ones around me. I would say horrible cuss words to my husband and even his grandfather that tried to talk to me. He has since passed away right around this time. My husband would hold me up against the wall and say look at me Heather. He would try to get the inner me to come back out and fight this demon within me.

Revelation 12:9 And the great dragon was cast out,that old serpent, called the Devil, and Satan, which deceiveth the whole world: he was cast out into the earth, and his angels we cast out with him.

Fighting a demon within you is tiring mentally and physically. When my husband aunt and uncle prayed over me for almost 45 minutes to rebuke the demon out I remember being so tired and hurting. It was as if I just got over the flu. My neck was sore from turning my head side to side. Throat was sore from screaming and speaking in a demonic language. My oldest son was there witnessing this, and he said all he seen was red eyes and my tongue was green. So believe what you may, but this is a true story.

I hope and pray that writing this book will change your mind about what you believe. If you study the Bible, you will know these things happen and are true. Many people are spiritual blind and do not want to open their eyes to evil things that can happen. There are evil spirits around you and you have to rebuke them in the name of Jesus Christ. Now I will continue onto my story.

James 2:19 Thou believest that there is one God; thou doest well: the devils also believe, and tremble.

Chapter

3

They Are Here!

My story goes back to March 2008. We had many unexplained things happen for the first time. In March, I was 6 months pregnant with my last child. My husband drove the family over to the Bonnie and Clyde trade days. While we were traveling over there, I noticed my seat belt was tugging on my stomach. At first, I thought it was the baby's movement. Then I thought it was my oldest son, setting in the rear, was tugging on the seat belt causing it to pull tighter on my stomach. I asked him if he was pulling on the seat belt. He said, "I am not doing anything!"

We got to the trade show and everything was normal whole day. I thought nothing more about it until we were returning home. The belt tugged on me as were driving. It pulled the belt tight over my pregnant stomach I had to take it off at one point to see why it did that. When I turned to grab the belt to put it back on it lashed at me and scared me. I saw then no one was even touching the seat belt. When we got home after a long and strange trip back, we went on as nothing had happened.

Months went by and nothing happened. I had our last child June 2008 and was a healthy baby boy. Things were normal for a while so it seemed. I now had a new born to take care along with two smaller children and my older one. I could not believe God had blessed us with four children. The doctor had told us we might not have any. Well God for sure had other plans for us. Being a mom of four children tired me out and I tried to nap when I could. There was a day in which I had a nap I will never forget.

It was July 2008 when things turned on my family for several weeks. I was laying down for a nap while my three younger kids were napping. My oldest son was on his PlayStation at the other end of our mobile home. Just as I was lying down, I woke up to a loud thump and then a breaking sounding at my bedroom door. I got up quickly and opened the door. My oldest son opened his door at the end of the hall and asked, "What was that?" I looked down, and there on the floor was one of my grandmother's old teapots. The pot had broken into many pieces in front at my bedroom door. I can tell they had thrown the teapot with force by sound and the break.

Let me say that this teapot was on the very top of my kitchen cabinets. There was no way possible it could slide off and move across my kitchen 19 feet away to my bedroom door. I measured, so it is an accurate distance for you to visualize how far it moved across the room. After I cleaned the broken teapot up, I tried to lie back down to ignore what had happened. I fell back to sleep but not for long. This spirit loves to play the fear game, and it wanted to play.

Again, I heard another sound from the kitchen. I opened my bedroom door to find my other teapot on the stove burner. It was not even broke. I moved it back to where I had it, which was up on top of the kitchen cabinet. I tried to take a nap once again. Moments later, I heard a loud thump but no breaking sound. I opened door again, it had thrown the same teapot across the kitchen, and broke the handle off. Both teapots came from my grandmother that passed away in October 2004.

The focus seemed to be on items that I had inherited or pictures of deceased relatives. At first, we thought my Grandmother came back as a spirit or my Mother was visiting us. Both had died recently. The activity began subtly but quickly intensified. We solely did not know what was going on! We must have made the dead angry, or they surely wanted to get our attention.

After they (Spirits) threw the teapots off the top of my kitchen cabinets, I took everything I had up there and moved them down. I was getting scared and did not understand what was going on. With this happening I could not go back to sleep. I called my husband and told him something strange is going on in our home. Even called his Grandmother and she told me it was the house settling. House settling does not throw a teapot across the room! We had been in our mobile home over 11 years at this time. It was as if she did not believe me. Therefore, I ignored what had happened. That idea did not last long because this spirit had more plans to scare us even more.

Later the spirit ran out of teapots to break so it focused on other things. Some days in your life, you remember very clearly. Tuesday, July 8, 2008 is one of those days. It is the day I felt some kind of spirit surrounding me. It was a very strange feeling, which is difficult to describe. I can say it was like cool air blowing around your body. Remember the devil can deceive you. At this time, I thought the Holy Spirit was what I was feeling. I felt the spirit continuing to surround me tighter and tighter. I had to do something. I was not sure if what I was feeling was good or evil so I grabbed my newborn thinking the spirit would stop. Boy was I wrong!

Job 4:15 Then a spirit passed before my face; the hair of my flesh stood up:

I was in my living room staring at my oldest son. It was as if I was in a trance. My eleven-year-old noticed I could not move or say anything. Then something pushed through my back and astounded me. We continued looking at each other without speaking. He realized something was wrong. I felt paralyzed or frozen and could not move. Strangest feeling I ever had in my life. This scared me to death.

Moments later, I could breathe normal again. I returned to my awareness and set down to catch my breath and contemplate what happened. I felt hope it was a good spirit but time would show it was not. Bad luck continued to follow me just as it had done for years prior.

Soon after that bad spirit went through me, I felt different. My personality changed to be a meaner person. I was home alone with my kids while my husband was at work. I was holding my newborn in my arms and I told my oldest son to come get the baby out of my arms I cannot move! I felt unsafe in my own home. I was not sure about how to handle this. The fear was overwhelming me.

Job 4:14   Fear came upon me, and trembling, which made all my bones to shake.

As I was standing in the middle of the living room, I had seen from the side of my eye my canisters on the kitchen counter slide across the counter. I was in shock and could not move from the fear. This spirit was out to put fear in me and it was working. I was so scared I called my husband and told him to come home now! Called my in laws over to see what was happening. When they got there, they were in disbelief of the occurrences. They too were finally seeing what I told them was happening.

Over the next few weeks and months, pictures fell off the wall. All of them did not fall in one day or at one time frame. They fell at various times. My Grandmother-in-law kept saying the mobile home was settling. The pictures hung very well onto the wall. I could not see how they could fall because of the foundation moving slightly. A spiritual thing happened that no one could certainly explain by foundation movement.

This was real things happening and you could not see what was moving the stuff. Spirits are things you cannot see with the eyes but can feel. Living in my home for the next several weeks and months was like living in a movie that was not real. Later I could distinguish between good and evil spirits. Being demon possessed and having Holy Spirit in you are two different feelings.

Demon spirit attacks you from behind and feels like it is pressing down. You are not able to breathe. Like a heavy oppression. It brings horrible words out of your mouth. I actually spoke in a demonic voice too. That is scary stuff! Holy Spirit comes from your belly with a cool breeze and chills sensation. You then become warm and free and then the heavenly language comes out of your mouth. You have a sense of peace and calm.

John 15:26 But when the Comforter is come, whom I will send unto you from the Father, even the Spirit of truth, which proceedeth from the Father, he shall testify of me:

John 15:27 And yeah shall bear witness, because ye have been with me from the beginning.

When things would randomly happen, I was able to tell where the demons would hide. Somehow being possessed and having Holy Spirit gave me the ability to find them. I could walk through my home and feel the negative energy in certain areas. It always seems to be stronger in my sons' room. Not sure, why it liked to stay in that room, but a lot of energy felt in there. When I would find it and prayed it out, it would go through the home and move things. It really was stupid because I would know it was still in the home.

Praying a demon out of a home is tiring. You will fight them for a while. Demons with hide from you too, until you start praying. While praying a demon out I always would open my front door to let it out of the home. I do that to show it who is boss of the home. You have to take authority of your home and not show fear. Demons will torment you longer if you show fear. They feed off it. In the past 11 years, I have learned when they show the lurking heads. My own kids can even tell when they are back. One of my sons has the ability to feel things as well. They too have seen, heard, and felt things.

Chapter

4

Spirits Says No Pictures

I t was all quiet on the battlefront with the unknown spirits in our home. Time passed and life marched on without incident and then they attacked in earnest.

Religion had always played a role in our family life. Our oldest son saved on June 19, 2008. He wanted to do it for months and finally just did it. I was proud of him deciding on his own. They baptized him on June 22, 2008. He had attended church by himself because I had stopped going. It had been four years since I had been to church. Perhaps, that was an invitation to the evil spirits that were soon attacking us.

On July 2004, once again, I was saved and baptized into the church. However, I stopped going after my Grandmother died in October 2004. I have to do a lot of soul searching to find cause for not attending church. It must have been anger over losing my Mother, Grandmother, and Grandfathers between 1993 and 2004. I felt abandoned, alone and sad. I miss them all. Losing all my close loved ones made me feel lost and confused. I had lost the ones that were helping guide me in life. Now whom do I turn to?

I found out I was pregnant with my first son four days after my Mother passed in 1996. I got pregnant with my second child, a girl, two months after my Grandmother passed in 2004. My Grandfather-in-law, who was a witness to some of the things that happened, passed in July 2008. That was six weeks after I gave birth to my last son. I felt I was nothing but bad luck to my family. At least no one died when I had my other son in 2006! I came to realize that God has a plan and life happens, as HE wants it. Before we are born or conceived, God has a plan for our lives. He even knows how many hairs are on our body.

Luke 12:7 But even the very hairs of your head are all numbered. Fear not therefore: yea are of more value than many sparrows.

With all my family that had passed away, I had wondered if they were the spirits. I used to think people could come back from the dead but I know that is not true. It says in the Bible we are all sleep until Jesus comes back if that is the case then the dead are sleep and not alive. I do not believe after going through this experience that one cannot come back to haunt you. Demons are liars and professional manipulators. They play games with your mind. So beware and do not be deceived.

Weeks after my oldest son dedication to God, the evil spirits decide it was time to show me who was boss. As I said before, they like to play games and they played many games well. On July 7, 2008 I was about to take a nap with my young daughter. Yes another nap scene, seems like they do not want you to sleep. Remember I had three small children and older child too. Moms are always tired when you take care of kids. In my case, I was taking care of them and coping with demons too. Children are a lot easier.

It was around 3:15 PM. My baby boy and my other young son were already napping. My older son was in his room, with the door closed, at the end of the hallway. I was looking forward to a short nap to rest after taking care of the kids all day. Nevertheless, the mean old demons had other plans to disrupt our lives even more.

We got in bed and it was less than 15 minutes when we heard a noise. It sounded like sounds I heard before and forced a fear I did not want again. I got up to go see what it could be. As I thought, a picture had fallen. My son came out of his room in response to the sound of the picture falling. Hoping it was just a fluke, I rehung the picture. I went back to my bedroom and lay down to resume the nap. My son returned to his room and shut his door.

It was about 10 minutes and an even louder sound can from the hall. This time the same picture had fallen and another one as well. Having rehung the first one that fell, I know it should not have fallen again. The other picture that fell was on the opposite hall wall. The first picture could never have hit the second picture to make it fall. It was obvious that we were about to have a visitor we could not see. Hoping for the best, I hung both pictures back on the wall to make sure their hung securely in place. I returned to get the nap I so wanted but my mind feared the worse. Moments after I lie down and even louder noise came from the hall. This time the two that fell and another one lay on the floor. One had a broken glass.

Not allowing the ghost to win, I again hung the pictures and waited in the living room watching the pictures. My greatest fear happen, all three pictures fell off the wall as I watched! I was now scared. I needed help. I called my Mother-in-law and her husband in a panic. They came and stayed more than one hour. Nothing happened, and they blew it off as settlement again.

After they left, the pictures fell from the wall again. I called them again, but they said it was just settlement and provided no help. I was getting angry and scared. The dang house was NOT settling. Something I cannot see was doing this. My husband would not be home until after 10 PM. It was getting dark outside and our fear of the dark just made it worse. To stop the ghost, we removed all pictures from the walls and waited for my husband to get home. He arrived and found all the lights on in the house. After my husband arrived, the strange event stopped.

So what was important about these pictures? Did something knock the pictures off the wall or were the pictures powerful enough they jumped off the wall? Whatever kind of spirit was in our home was not a happy one. It wanted me to believe it was a loved one coming back from the dead to torment us. I knew better than that!

1 Thessalonians 4:16 For the Lord himself shall descend from heaven with a shout, with the voice of the archangel, and with the trump of God: and the dead in Christ shall rise first.

I decided to keep my pictures down since the demons kept knocking them down. I got tired of picking them up and broken glass as well. We kept all pictures stored until we got control of the destructive demons. We have had many things broken. They have broken picture frames, teapots, CDs, glasses, mini blinds, and ceiling fan. As you can tell, we had angry and mean demons in our home. They were out to torment us.

Chapter

5

The Spirits Get Angry

I have a picture of my Mother: that I mentioned passed away in September 1996. It was one of my favorite pictures of her. She looked so pretty with long dark brown hair. I cherished this picture. However, when this demon showed back up, it made me hate the picture suddenly. Things started happening again in the house.

We thought this picture was the problem, so we had removed it from the home. However, later found the picture was not the issue. I felt the need to include the picture of my mom in this book to show it was just an ordinary picture. Keep in mind demons love to deceive us as human beings. They will use loved ones to deceive you.

When I looked at it, I felt I could not stand to see it. I had difficulty with breathing when I viewed the picture! So my son and I got back to back. I could not see the picture being in this position. He would then turn the picture towards him and I felt something come through me and could not breathe. When he turned the picture away from him, I was fine like nothing happened. We repeated this with the same results. It was freaking me out, and I thought I was going crazy.

Thinking it was the picture causing all the problems, I had my son take it to the storage shed. Not having many pictures of my deceased Mother, I did not want to destroy it. I hoped by removing it from the house the activity would stop. I base this assumption on a story told to me by my Grandmother. This is not the first time my Mother has appeared in the spirit form.

2 Corinthians 11: 13 For such are false apostles, deceitful workers, transforming themselves into the apostles of Christ.

I wrote my Dad an email that told this story told to me by my Grandmother. To set the stage, Debbie is my Mother, Herman is my step-dad, Nanny is my Grandmother, and Beth is my sister. Her story begins with...............

Nanny in the bedroom asleep: "She was waked up about 2 AM in the morning to go to the bathroom. When she came out of the bathroom she noticed the living room that is on one end of the kitchen area of her apartment was brighter than normal. As if a light had been left on. She did not pay a lot of attention because the entrance to the apartment drive is straight in front of her living room window. Anyone driving in would shine light into the room at night. She thought someone left the living room light on so when she turned to go down the small hallway she noticed Mama (Debbie) and Herman sitting at her kitchen table. Mama was sitting there smiling and had her dark blue blanket over her as she had on when they showed her body at the funeral home on a table. Herman had his suit on that he was wearing when he had his funeral. Mama did not say anything the whole time, but Herman said to Nanny, "What are we going to do about Beth?" and Nanny said, "I don't know!" Herman said, "Well you don't worry about Beth because I will be watching over her and she will be ok." Then Mama and Herman got up and Mama's hand came out from underneath the blanket and grabbed Herman's hand and they walked out into the living room window and then it went very dark in the room. After it turned dark then Nanny said the room got really cold!" Nanny and step grandpa, heard voices. They entered the room to find no one there. He found Nanny was terribly upset from what she had seen. He comforted her and went back to bed and that was the story. The people she had just seen had been dead for months. It was not long after the incident my step grandpa became ill in the apartment. He later died there of a stroke. Nanny moved out after his death. It was too much for her to handle being in a place where he died. It would not be long after he died that death knocked on my Nanny's door. She suffered a stroke, but did not suffer from pain at the end. Nanny was in a nursing home the last time I seen her alive.

She also said she has had other strange things happen after my Mom died. I also told this story in the same email to my Dad.

"The other thing that had been happening to Nanny was the picture on her bedroom wall above the bed. She would be in a deep sleep and woken up by a bumping sound and she could not figure out where it was coming from. She would get up and turned the light on and it would stop. For a while each night it would do this and she would get up, turn the light on and once again it would stop. Her and Papaw finally got up one night and looked all over the bedroom trying to find that bumping sound. Then they determined the sound was coming from the picture on the wall above their bed. They turned the light on, Nanny placed her hand on the picture, and it was warm to the touch. The air conditioner and a fan were on in the room and it was cool in the bedroom but the picture was warm. The picture would bump every night for a long time and Nanny was getting scared from it. Papaw told her, "Don't be scared Debbie is trying to tell you something." However, they did not know what it could be. Anyways the picture keep bumping and being warm until Nanny had moved out of the apartment and into her trailer and it never did that again. I now have that picture! Nanny also said since grandpa (ghostly spirit) has died he would tickle her feet while she would try to go to sleep. Her bed would move as if someone was getting in it. She said it is Papaw sleeping with her every night. But

after her and Wolf has been seeing each other he (Papaw) doesn't do it anymore... don't know if his ghostly spirit is mad at her or he feels like Nanny has moved on without him.

Nanny could not secure the picture enough to stop the occurrences, so she gave the picture to me. The picture is the one mention in the earlier part of this book. It seems to play a role in all the activities by the spirit including the one now occurring to my oldest son. My Mother had her problems when she was alive and surly took those problems with her in death.

I know my mom was no saint. However, nobody is. She had many faults in her life and made many mistakes. She had never attended church in her younger days. I do not recall her ever going to be honest. Nevertheless, I can say during her last days of her life she was attending church. I have had one of my sisters ask me do I think she went to heaven. She believed in God and I would think she went to heaven. Only way, I would ever know is when my time comes.

We also had another experience with a different picture. My son had an 8 x 10 picture of Jesus in his room. I saw the picture and instantly had the feeling of something rushing through me taking my breath. I stopped looking at it and breathing returned to normal. When I would see the picture, I got disgusted. I hated looking at the picture of Jesus of all things. It shocked me.

Then I saw the Bible on his dresser and again the spirit rushed through me! Once again, I felt disgusted looking at the Bile. I tried to hold the picture of Jesus and the Bible and could not. Something forced it out of my hand and threw it down to the floor. I could not understand what was going on. Clearly, something was wrong here.

I decided it was not my Mother's picture, which was not the problem. I had him go back to the storage building and bring my picture back. That turned out to be a bad idea. This demon does not like my son or me. It seems like it has issues with us. This is why him and me had to take over together to fight this demon later on.

2 Corinthians 11:14 And no marvel; for Satan himself is transformed into an angel of light.

Chapter

6

Angry Poltergeists

The trip to the storage house did not take long. My son ran back in the house hysterical. He was screaming and crying. Freaked out by what he saw in the shed. He could barely speak or breathe being very distraught. Shortly, he could finally tell what happened. He said, "I was thrown out of the storage building!" I said, "What do you mean you got thrown out?" He said, "Something picked me up off the floor and threw me out the door!"

In addition, he saw something in the shed. While being thrown in the air, he saw someone looking at him. He said it was my Mother in a blue shirt and blue pants with short curly hair. He said she was looking right at him while being lifted up in the air and thrown out of the shed. How do you explain that you just seen someone that is dead? People do not just appear from the dead. I was in total disbelief of what my son was telling me. This all sounded too crazy to believe.

We were talking in the kitchen where we had a clear view out the window of the storage shed. While telling me what happened, he looked toward the shed and again freaked out. He said, "Look Mom!" She is still out there! He was looking at my Mother in a blue shirt and blue pants again! This time her hair was shoulder length and wavy just as it was before she died. Once again, she was looking directly at him. He said, "Do you see her?" I said, "NO!"

Once believed that stone, wood, and articles owned by the deceased will trigger the deceased spirit that had owned them. The wood used to build the shed came from the house where my Mother had lived. This house now dismantled and rebuilt into my dad's new old house. Which he at times has paranormal activity as well. I will enlighten you more later in the story about that. This may have produced a large trigger object according to some ghost hunters.

She then disappeared, and he felt this spirit go though him. He had the picture of her in one hand and his other hand was trying to get the picture from his hand! Something was controlling his hand. Being in the kitchen, I pushed him in the corner of my kitchen cabinets and held him while I grabbed the Bible. I put my Bible on his head and tried to get the picture out of his hand. He was fighting me and he was very strong! Finally, he became himself again, and I let go. He was crying and did not know what was going on.

We both looked outside to see if my Mom was still outside anywhere. We did not see her anymore. However, when we were looking for her, we saw something else. My oldest son said, "Mom I see a purple snake out in the woods!" I said, "A what?" He said it again, and I looked outside and saw nothing at first. Then I looked again and seen a set of yellow evil eyes looking at me! I could not believe my eyes!

Moments after seeing the yellow eyes in the woods my son said, "Mom I see the purple snake coming towards the house!" It wanted to come in! I told him we were not letting it in. Well it made its way through the house and went to the back yard. I never seen the purple snake as he did I just seen the yellow eyes in the woods. After we saw, it and it went through the house it left. Was another weird thing to experience and see? Well there is a lot more to tell in the story. As I said before, after reading my story, you should become a believer of the paranormal spirits.

1 John 4:1 Beloved, believe not every spirit, but try the spirits whether they are of God: because many false prophets are gone out into the world.

After all this happened we were very scared, so I called my doubting Grandmother-in-law for help and to stay until my husband returned from work. My husband collects many CDs. We store them in the living room on the wall next to the kitchen. When my Grandmother-in-law arrived, she set in the recliner to wait for my husband. Just as she was setting down, the CDs starting flying out of the bookshelf. They flew over her head scaring her. They were not one or two but fifty of more were flying over her head.

A can of corn was setting on the kitchen counter. The spirit did not like her so threw it and tried to hit her head. Luckily, the ghost was not much of a pitcher and did not harm her. Pictures then flew off the walls to the floor. She was so scared and shocked she prayed Jesus name loudly. As grandmother kept repeating Jesus, the demon got more violent. She was always saying it was just the house settling but not now! She was a true believer now. It was just another day living with spirits but we were scared at the power of this ghost.

1Timothy 4:1 Now the Spirit speaketh expressly, that in the latter times some shall depart from the faith, giving heed to seducing spirits, and doctrines of evils;

I picked up the pictures but the spirit would just throw them on the floor again. I thought this was over or I would not but the picture back up. Therefore, I left them on the floor again. I could not believe what I was seeing! I had never experienced such power from the spirit and freaked out. My one-year-old son and two-year-old daughter were seeing all this. They thought we were playing, and this was funny to have things fly around the room. I was not laughing, I was crying.

Revelation 16:14 For they are the spirits of devils, working miracles, which go forth unto the kings of the earth and of the whole world, to gather them to the battle of that great day of God Almighty.

My kids were young when all this was going on. They do not remember all this. However, as time went by and when things would happen later in years to come I had to tell them about this. For them to understand what was happening they must know. All my kids have experienced the paranormal. No my family or kids are not crazy people either. Since my kids, gotten older people ask them about this stuff. Some believe and some do not. Some are scared, and some are intrigued.

I tell my kids to tell the truth of what happen. I do not care what others may think of us. We have been through a lot in past 11 years. This story is of truth. Today we still will experience little things but we just ignore it. The saying is if you do not entertain, it will stop. When kids were younger, they would entertain not knowing what they are playing with. We do not know when it my start again.

1 Peter 5:8 Be sober, be vigilant; because your adversary the devil, as a roaring lion, walketh about, seeking whom he may devour.

Example of this is one time I walked into their room and clothes was everywhere. I got mad because they emptied every dresser draw. Clothes were even hanging on the light fixture in the ceiling. I would ask how this happen and they would say I do not know. During this same time, I noticed red marker all over my wall. Of course they do not know who did that either. Demons are like dangerous little kids you have to show them who are boss.

I mentioned things can be trigger objects and my Dad had some paranormal activity in his home. After his Grandmother died, there appeared a blue ball of light in his library. It came out of the 1950s magazines setting midways in a bookcase. Went toward him and turned to travel thru the floor. It never returned. While running a Ghost program on his iPhone, in the same room, it indicated the words Debbie and Beth. This was when Beth was in the hospital and was very ill. It was as if Debbie was asking someone to help her daughter, Beth.

Chapter

7

Attempts To Remove Spirit

The activity was so fierce I felt I had to get help from the church. I called my son's preacher, and he came over with some church members. This preacher has since moved off and could not interview him for more information of what he saw. My Grandmother-in-law called her pastor as well to come and help. He since then passed away. They arrived when the activity had stopped but saw the mess it had created. They helped clean up the glass and vacuumed the floors.

My son's preacher walked into my home the first time and asked, "Do you have any movies with magic or demonic things in them?" I told him we do. He asked us to remove them from the house. The preacher asked me about one particular movie. We gave it to him and he took it to the church and left it there overnight. He even tried to burn it for us but it would not burn. Days later in a large fire, we burned it ourselves along with other movies and books. We hoped it was over but now it attacked in a new way. It wanted me!

Acts 19:19 Many of them also which used curious arts brought their books together, and burned them before all men: and they counted the price of them, and found it fifty thousand pieces of silver.

While the preacher and the church members were at my house, they had me read from the Bible aloud. They had me read in Romans about salvation. I started to read and found I could not say the word "Jesus". I was so shocked! Something confused me and could not understand why I could not say the words from the Bible. Then, thru me, a demonic spirit talked to them.

Luke 8:30 And Jesus asked him, saying, What is thy name? And he said, Legion: because many devils were entered into him.

The church group asked it, "What is your name?" It would not tell them. The demon spirit said, "I want to kill her and I am not letting her go?" The voice I spoke was in a man's voice during this. They tried to get me to hold the Bible and the Jesus picture again. I could not hold the Bible or look at a picture of Jesus. I did not know what was happening. The worse thing is you remember what you are saying and doing while possessed. However, you have no control. It is as if you are watching a movie. I had seen things like this in movies and it was now happening to me!

As strange as it seems, the demon spirit would come and go into me. I would be fine one minute and the next I am possessed again. I knew when it would happen to me because I could feel the presence of the spirit as it came toward me. I knew exactly where it was and when it came in me. It is hard to explain the feeling. I know it is not the same feeling you feel once saved. That is a feeling of joy and relief of burdens. The demon spirit feeling is fear and horror. It is a mistake to ask a demon to come to you. You can easily tell the difference between the demon spirit and Holy Spirit.

At one point of this day, I was talking to my sister on the phone. We both thought it might be our Mother doing all this stuff. She was no angel while living. My sister had me hold up the phone in the air. She was talking to the spirit. She told it to leave me along and come after her. That is a brave thing to say but also not very smart when dealing with the unknown. The next thing I know, my sister's voice changed. She screamed that something was coming thru the phone after her. I could feel the spirit in the phone too. It was crazy. I was standing in the middle of my living room with all these people watching me as I was hollering at this spirit to get out of my phone.

Finally, someone took the phone from me and disconnected the call to my sister. One of the men from the church said there was nothing in the phone. I told him, "Yes there was!" I felt the presence of this thing thru the phone! He clarified he did not believe me and never came back to our house. It was clear he thought I was not right (crazy) and that was the problem, not a ghost. We all have opinions, and his is wrong.

I wanted people to believe me and see for themselves. I know what I was feeling and seeing. God, my family, and I know it was happening. Unfortunately, my husband's grandparents have both passed as well. It would be good if others believed me but unnecessary. I am writing this book, not for me, but because I feel God would want me to tell others about evil spirits. They are real. This book is for you. Most importantly, this book is for God.

Things finally calmed down that afternoon. The preachers prayed over me hoping to stop the attacks. They anointed our home with oil and prayer. We walked throughout the house putting oil over the windows and doors as they prayed. All thought it was over and went home. They were wrong. When you argue with a demon, a few words from the Bible and a little olive oil will not do the job. The oil should be the proper blessed anointing oil.

Luke 10:21 Behold, I give unto you power to tread on serpents and scorpions, and over all the power of the enemy: and nothing shall by any means hurt you.

Later that night things started back up. In desperation, I called the preachers back. They returned and prayed over me and anointed the home with oil again. They were not Catholic so holy water not used to clean the house. No sage or salt spread around the room as some suggest. The religious actions taken seemed to calm the demon but not remove.

I tried reading the Bible in an attempt to be saved, but could not read it. The group prayed and the demons attack on me seemed to stop again. I again attempted to read the Bible with success. I hoped it was finally over! A person with hope and nothing else is a person continuing to search for more their entire life. We needed more than hope. We need faith that God will help us overcome this demon.

By late night of the second day, everything had calmed down. Fear of the unknown remained. My son placed his mattress on the floor of our room because of that fear. He wanted to sleep close to his parents. Before going to bed that night we placed all our Bibles on the kitchen table. My son placed a Bible under his pillow on the floor for protection. He placed his clothes at his bedside. The bedroom door was close, but I knew it would never keep a spirit out.

Every time I needed to make a bottle for our newborn, I would wake up my husband to go with me. Later I got smart and brought stuff to make the bottles in my bathroom. I did not want to walk into the kitchen alone. Demons want to put fear in you and fear I had. At times, I froze from the fear especially at night.

I had the worst time sleeping. I kept feeling my cover pulled on. It felt as if someone was messing with my hair. I even felt someone poke my arm, and these was no one there! It felt like the longest night of my life. Everyone else slept comfortable all night. I kept being waking up with something bothering me all night long. Worst sleep I ever had. This demon was making me feel like a crazy person.

It was Wednesday, July 9, 2008. We all woke up, my son noticed his Bible, and clothes were missing. We looked around the room and could not find his things. Therefore, my husband opened the door and saw his clothes in the kitchen. His shirt was on the highchair and his shorts were on the kitchen floor. We walked further into the room and noticed the Bibles on the table placed in a shape of a cross on the table. That shocked us! Strangely, we found my son's Bible in the dresser drawer in our bedroom. We never heard the door or drawer open and close.

John 10:10 The thief cometh not, but for to steal, and to kill, and to destroy: I am come that they might have life, and that they might have it abundantly.

I do not know when the Bible moved. I know my son's clothes were still in the bedroom around 7 AM that morning. I was up feeding the baby and saw his things in the bedroom where he left them. I went back to sleep, and we all woke up about 8 AM. The demon spirit had moved the Bible and clothes between 7 AM and 8 AM. All moved without making any sounds. This was the beginning of another long day of demon horror.

Chapter

8

Demon Is In Me

After we got up; I had strange feelings. I was feeling the demon spirit coming around me again. It would come and go through me. At one point, it stayed in me. My husband had to hold me against the wall while I was speaking to him in another voice. I (it) cursed him. I (it) told my husband it would kill me that my husband did not love me, and he could not have me back. I remember hitting my head against the wall trying to hurt myself. Then it stopped again. I cried, "Oh God what is happening to me?" I had never been so scared in my life!

Then it would come around me again and I would scream at it. I said, "No! No! Get away from me!" Then it would come back in me again. It was a fight I could not win by myself. Being alone when a spirit comes around is even more frightening!

My husband had a business meeting he had to attend. Therefore, we called family members over and the preachers. The preachers were busy and could not come until later. My Grandparents-in-law, Mother-in-law and her husband, and Brother-in-law came to help me while my husband was gone. My husband's uncle and aunt also came to help with this demon possession. They were here the day before but nothing happened. They would not be disappointed this time.

While waiting on family members to arrive, my oldest son wanted to try to get me to read the Bible. We tried in one room then another. Finally, we tried in his bedroom while he held the 8 x 10 picture of Jesus. While doing this I still could not read the Bible. I did not want to hold the Bible and look at the picture of Jesus. Demons as you know cannot stand God's word or His face.

The demon spirit within was getting stronger by the time my relatives arrived. Today the aunt and uncle are alive and probably can still tell about this if asked. When they walked into my son's room, my eyes got so big and I screamed. I yelled for them to leave me along. The demon knew he met his match. Then, the next thing I know I was speaking in a demonic language. I did not know a tongue could move that fast. In response, they spoke back in tongues (Holy Spirit) telling the demon to get out of me. I (it) was fighting to stay inside and spit at them. What a radical split personality! They had to hold me down to keep from hitting them. My son was on the floor with the Jesus picture watching all this craziness.

Acts 2:3 And there appeared unto them cloven tongues like as of fire, and it sat upon each of them.

My son should have not witnessed all this, but he did. Being eleven-year-old boy things like this can traumatize a child. However, my son seemed to be intrigued. He asked to stay in the room to try to help. He felt like him holding the picture of Jesus would get rid of the demon himself. He was wrong it took someone with the Holy Spirit to do an exorcism on me. So therefore, we had to call in reinforcements that helped him.

Acts 2:4 And they were all filled with the Holy Ghost, and began to speak with other tongues, as the Spirit gave them utterance.

At one point, the demon tried to hide itself in me. My aunt said, "I know you're still there, get out of here you liar!" I said," I am fine now." Then I looked into her eyes and it started up again. It tried hiding but with her Holy Spirit guidance, she knew better. They were praying in tongues with Godly language, while I spoke demonic. This went on what seems liked forever. It took my husband's aunt and uncle over 30 minutes for them to rebuke the demon out of me. They told me it was a strong demon in me so it was difficult to remove. My body had gone through a wringer. My neck, back, and even my face were sore for days. I felt as if I had exercised for many hours. That was the worst thing I ever experienced in my life.

Later my son told me that my tongue was green, my eyes were dark red, and white foam from the mouth when I was possessed. This was not a pretty sight for the family to see. In addition, he was not even scared. I confirmed the look from my husband's aunt. She agreed with his overview of my looks. I am so glad I did not see myself in a mirror or in a reflection of someone's glasses. I could never get the vision out of my head if I had seen me that way.

After the exorcism was over, I was completely drained and very thirsty. I had the worse sore throat ever. I felt the oppression lifted off my shoulders. I was very tired. It even drained my husband's aunt and uncle. Once we got up, we all went into the living room. I told them I felt the need to be saved right then. Therefore, I brought a chair into the middle of the living room and I sat in it. They begin praying over me and asking me to repeat Romans 10:9-13 with them. I did. I felt a big relief come over me.

I figured everything would be over for good once saved. Things went back to normal it seemed. Felt I could breathe for the first time in a while. The atmosphere was calm feeling. I did not even feel any presence of a demon anymore. However, you have to keep your guard up at all times. Demons will hide and come back out when least expected.

To fight a demon, one must put on the armor of God as the Bible states. Writing verses from King James Version of my bible to show what it says about what the Armor of God is. I hope this will help in your fight against the devil.

Ephesians 6:11 Put on the whole armor of God, that ye may be able to stand against the wiles of the devil.

I will list seven things I feel will help fight this battle.

1. Belt of truth Ephesians 6:14

2. Breastplate of righteousness Ephesians 6:14

3. Feet fitted with the gospel of peace Ephesians 6:15

4. Shield of faith Ephesians 6:16

5. Helmet of salvation Ephesians 6:17

6. Sword of the Spirit 2 Ephesians 6:17

7. Pray in the Spirit on all occasions

Ephesians 6:17 And take the helmet of salvation, and the sword of the Spirit, which is the word of God.

Salvation Prayer:

Romans10:9 That is thou confess with thy mouth the Lord Jesus, and shalt believe in thine heart that God hath raised from the dead, thou shalt be saved. 10 For with the heart man believeth unto righteousness; and with the mouth confession is made unto salvation. 11 For the scripture saith, Whosever believeth on him shall not be ashamed. 12 For there is no difference between the Jew and the Greek: for the same Lord over all is rich unto all that call upon him. 13 For whosever shall call upon the name of the Lord shall be saved.

Chapter

9

God Sends Help

After the day ended, we thought everything was fine. Everyone went home. Nothing happened the rest of the night. We decided there was safety in numbers. Therefore, we placed a mattress on the living room floor to camp out there. We got ready for bed and slept all night with the television playing Christian music. For a few days, we felt safe sleeping this way. Peace and quiet never lasts long when you have a monster living in your house.

When we woke up, it was now Thursday, July 10, 2008. We thought everything was fine; the insanity was over. It was a very nice summer day. That night my son was setting at the kitchen table reading the Bible. I looked over at him and he was just staring at the Bible. I said his name several times before he looked up at me. He had a strange look on his face. I asked if he was OK. He replied, "Yes".

I had a bookmark on the table beside him. It had an angle and a little girl on it. He was staring at the bookmarker. I watched him put his finger on the bookmarker's picture. His hand shook when he placed his finger on it. He to my amazement he pointed at the Bible and the page turned without him touching it. Was this a gift or something else?

He had me put my finger on the bookmarker and my finger shook too. However, I could not turn the pages as he had done. I felt something around us. I knew then that our home still had the demonic spirits and not cleansed.

Galatians 6:7 Be not deceived; God is not mocked: for whatsoever a man soweth, that shall he also reap.

I have a picture of my deceased Grandmother stuck on my refrigerator next to a Jesus magnet. My son had me touch both at the same time and I could feel a spirit around me. I was very close to my Grandmother. I felt it might be her but unless I see or hear the spirit, I cannot know.

Oh well, I walked from the kitchen towards the living room. Then, I heard my name called in my Grandmother's voice. She said, "Heather." I stopped from the shock of what I heard. Her voice was a one of a kind with no possible mistake in knowing it was she. I turned and faced the kitchen and asked, "Nanny (My Grandmothers nick name) is that you?" Generally you can hear or/and feel spirits but not see them. I did not see anything, but I felt the spirit come toward me. I did not back away or run from it, I allowed it to touch me, to hug me. I felt her arms wrap around me but I could not see anything. Who can say a spirit has hugged them? The hug dissipated and she was gone. Now I know she has been watching as I thought.

If that was not strange enough, what follows is an event that should be placed in the "too strange to be believed" records. After she left, my son, and I felt others around us. We started to feel many. They were like unseen round balls of energy. They are like the orbs my camera has been photographing in the house. There were so many and distinctively separate that we could hold them in our hands but not see them. Then we could toss them to each other. I have to admit, I find this difficult to believe as well. If you could not catch it, it hit you in the stomach and you bent over slightly from the gentle impact. It did not hurt from the impact. You saw nothing but felt them.

The spirits were not at rest this day. That evening my son asked if I could see the little redheaded boy by the couch. I said, "What boy?" I saw nothing. Balls of spirit energy, a Grandmother ghost, and now a little boy ghost. There must be a portal inside our home to have this type of supernatural activity or both of us are crazy.

My son said the little boy was about 10 years old and was an angel. Then he said more angels were arriving. He said, "There are baby angels everywhere! Do you see them?" I said, "I don't see anything, but I feel them. As my son said, they appeared to be everywhere. I could feel them as I walked thru them. The room was getting crowded as a few tall male angels also arrived. He said the men angels were very tall, over six feet.

Matthew 24:4 And Jesus answered and said unto them, Take heed that no man deceive you.

This was weird so again I called for help from my family. From our insane description of the events occurring, my brother-in-law and three friends rushed over to see. One of them was on the police force and one had had a temperature sensor. The sensor could measure hot and cold from a distance. Sadly, the sensor did not find irregularities in the room. Demons love to run and hide.

Matthew 24:5 For many shall come in my name, saying, I am Christ; and shall deceive many.

However, there were a few times when my brother-in-law came over and was hit with things. He can still today verify all this. Once he was walking out of our bathroom and a tube of toothpaste hit him in the back of his head. Another time he was walking through the living room and a TV remote hit him in the back of his head again. Demons love to attack from behind. My brother-in-law saw moving things but never seen or felt the spirit doing it.

Moreover, my mother-in-law saw a Destin tube thrown across the room along with many other things she saw. She was there when things moved and thrown as well and can verify the facts I write.

The real question was can they see or feel any of the activity? There were about twelve people in our house. My son and I wanted to see if we could throw those spirit balls around and have others feel them. Some said they could feel them and others could not. One of the girls that were there was able to feel the spirits and see them. She too wanted to throw some spirits to each other too. Sense the angels seemed to be friendly toward my son, she decided to ask them questions.

I do not recall what she asked but I know my son asked her a question. He asked her if she was pregnant. She freaked out over what he had asked and ran outside. How did he know she might have been pregnant? When she got into the car, my son said he could see a redheaded boy on top of the car. I later found out she was not pregnant but at this time she thought she might have been.

2 Corinthians 2:11 Lest Satan should get an advantage of us: for we are not ignorant of his devices.

Being that this happened over 11 years ago, the details of what happened next will be hard to tell. I have tried to contact some of the people that were there at this time. One moved away and other three cannot seem to remember any more than what I have written.

I understand that some of these sound unbelievable. I am writing what I remember to be the full truth. Finding the people that witness a lot of this is hard. Some have passed away, moved, or simply cannot remember. Telling the truth of this story with what I know if better than telling lies of what I do not know.

James 2:19 Thou believest that there is one God; thou doest well: the devils also believe, and tremble.

Chapter

10

Doves and Little Angels

Later, after everyone had left, we were watching TV.
We were listening to either preaching or Christian
music to help keep the demons away. So we thought. He
said to me, "Mom, I see a white dove!" I said, "I don't see
them!" However, I heard the ruffling of bird wings. My
son said he was seeing doves everywhere and grabbed
them. He would throw them toward me and I could feel
them go thru me. He held one and placed it on my arm. I
could feel it but not see it. With confidence, he opened his
hand and all the doves went into his palm. He shut his
hand. When he opened his hand, the doves would fly back
out.

We searched the house to see if there were other areas
having supernatural events. Arriving in the bathroom my
son said, "I feel something evil near the bathtub." He did
some type of hand motions, turned to me and announced
it was gone. Before leaving the bath, he saw feathers
everywhere. When he put his hand out to catch them, they
went into his hand. He would throw the feathers back out
and ask if I could see them. He said, "They are so pretty!"
Once again, I said, "I see nothing!" All the things my son

was saying he saw I never saw. I know he was truthful because I could hear flapping of the wings and could feel the wind on me from the feathers and it was all around me.

The same night we were sitting at the kitchen table talking and my son says, "The baby angels want us to read to them." Believing him, we got out our Children's Story Bible. We sat it on the table and it opened up to a story by itself. My son said he guessed they want to hear this story. It was late at night and everyone else was sleep. While he was reading to them, all my kitchen chairs slid out as if someone was setting down. We sit in two of the chairs and the other four slid over. I checked the chairs to be sure my son was not moving them, which he was not. He could not move several chairs at once.

2 Corinthians 11:13 For such are false apostles, deceitful workers, transforming themselves into the apostles of Christ.

The next thing I know, while setting at the table, I felt something around my feet. It felt like someone tickles them. My son said he was feeling the same thing. He said they want to play. When the little spirits touch you, it felt like an electric shock or a numbing and tingling feeling. I did not hurt, just a weird feeling. When I got up to walk, there were two little baby angels around the age of two or three. They wanted to hold my hands. I let them and you could feel that weird feeling as they touched you. It was good to have good spirits near instead of evil! However, later I find no spirits are good spirits!

I was getting tired. It was well after midnight. I told my son to tell the angels we had to go to sleep. He did a hand motion to tell them it was time for bed. He said, "Ok we can go to bed now. They want bother you now." The whole time these angels were around him he would do these and signals. I asked him, "Why are you doing the hand motions?" He told me that some baby angles were deaf and could not hear him. I guess those would not have listened to the Bible stories.

We finally made it to bed after a long day. While sleeping something was pulling my covers and slightly touching my hair. I did not sleep well. I do not know why the demon spirits always picked on me. Is it because I feared it? Maybe I did. Everyone else got a good sleep each night except me. If my son supposedly put these angels to sleep then who was bothering me while I was trying to sleep? You try sleeping with paranormal activity going on in your home. Bet you cannot.

HEATHER

Chapter

11

I Know Your Past

Late in the night of Saturday, July 12, 2008, things happened again. My son and I were in the living room watching a Christian channel. During a song, my son had his eyes closed and hands in the air. He shook and cried. I thought he was with the Holy Spirit, but that was not the situation. I asked him if he was all right. He said, "Yes, but something is different here!" I asked, "What do you mean, different?" He looked around at me and told me things about my past. Things he could not have known without being there himself. He then showed me he could tell me things about people by looking at their photos.

2 Timothy 3:13 But evil men and seducers shall wax worse and worse, deceiving, and being deceived.

I told him this gift was not from God. He should stop reading people's past from the pictures. I told him the devil was being deceitful. He was making you think this is a good thing to do. God would never want you to know things about people without their permission. He would especially not want you to know the bad things they have done. He knowing some things about us all was very disturbing. Once he knows this, he does not forget it. You never want your child knowing things of your past. They say your past can come back to haunt you and boy did it.

The next day, Sunday, July 13, 2008 my husband and I went to church for our baptism. Afterwards, we went to my husband's grandparent house. My son was still trying to read peoples past. I was getting upset and kept telling him to stop. He did not want to stop and became angry. We argued intensely. He became aggressive and wanted to fight! We had to hold him down until he calmed down. The anger made it clear the "gift" was not from God.

We again went to church services that night. While the members were singing, a terrible thunderstorm rumbled though knocking out electrical power to the whole community. The storm was unexpected. It seemed to say more bad is coming, get ready. I was hoping the storm was washing away the surrounding bad. Nevertheless, that was not the case.

As a precaution after the service that night, we had our preacher pray over our son. Based on his behavior we were worried he may be possessed too. He had no bad reaction to the preacher's prayer so things seemed ok. We, left traveling back home. Just as were thought, we also had no electrical power at the house. We stayed at my husband's grandparent house because of the hot weather.

During our power outage, I would never go into the house alone. I was too scared to go in without the lights on. So keep staying with the grandparents. However, even being over there, I still would feel things messing with me in my sleep. Therefore, this showed me that they do follow you. Nevertheless, why follow me?

Matthew 26:10 When Jesus understood it, he said unto them, Why trouble ye the woman? For she hath wrought a good work upon me.

The next morning, I went back home, but we still had no power. Therefore, we continued to stay at the grandparent's house for the day. Late evening the power returned, and we went home. My husband had been at work and he did not return until late that night. When he returned, I had all the lights on. When we came home, I felt the bad spirits were back and memories of the past battles came rushing back. I was just plain scared and felt the house was again not clean from the spirits.

From this point on, I cannot provide dates and times of all the events that happened. We would experience activity one day but not the next. I recall a time when our newborn son's pacifier found hung on my "angel plates". None of us put them there. We even had our pillows and blankets thrown around the living room. We still do not even have a ceiling fan to this day.

Another time I had a roast laid out in the kitchen sink. We found a knife in the sink and the roast sliced open. None of us had used the knife to make the cut. We had things like this go on for 41 days strong. We asked each other did you do this or that. Who threw that? Did you move this? It made you feel as if you were losing control of your mind.

The one thing I regret was not doing a better job of keeping notes about the major activates during the 41 days. I should have written everything down day to day. I was just plain so scared and not sure about what was going on. Because it was not an everyday occurrence, I did not write down the events. My Dad said these things do not happen to very many people. If you want to tell others, you need to take notes to get the facts on paper.

Millions of people have never seen a ghost or saw objects move on their on power. They have never experienced CD's flying around a room. I should have listened to his advice for my notes would have more detail of the 41 days of this. We have had many other experiences after this time but not this strong. The 41 days was the strongest, strangest, of the other days that would come. There was more horror to come.

I can tell you the demon and non-demon spirits are real. My family members have experienced them first hand. If only one person experienced these events, you might say they have an issue. However, when a family of six says it is true, you should believe them. I felt and heard the supernatural personally and up close. Have you ever been hugged by your dead grandmother? Have you ever felt an invisible dove on your arm? Maybe having to deal with a demon and angels is an experience many would like to have. As a mother of four living in a small mobile home, I could have been very happy to get just the hug without all the demon's activities.

John 8:44 Ye are of your father the devil, and the lusts of your father ye will do. He was a murderer from the beginning, and abode not in the truth,because there is no truth in him. When he speaketh a lie, he speaketh of his own: for he is a liar, and the father of it.

We had things thrown, moved, opened, and broke because of the demon spirits. When all of this started, we did not understand what was happening. We, as well as you, did not believe this could happen in real life. It only happened in the movies. Boy was I wrong and so are you. I was not strong enough to make the bad spirits leave. Two church preachers and members could not rid our home of them either. Who would have thought our son would be the one? He was only 11 years old and had experienced a lifetime of supernatural events. He was to be the hero of this story. He held the key to remove the evil within me and my home. So we thought.

Revelation 20:10 And the devil that deceived them was cast into the lake of fire and brimstone, where the beast and the false prophet are, and shall be tormented day and night forever more.

Chapter

12

Get Out!

I just made the decision to name this chapter; I typed it in above and went to type it in the table of contents. The title was typed in already, but not by me! Maybe the spirits wanted to make one final point--they "allow" me to write this book. You need to know they are only an invitation away, waiting for you to do something stupid and invite them. I know they are watching and waiting for a chance to enter my life or yours. We battled them for many months and now, on a special day, they left.

The special day of cleansing is an exact date is unknown, but it was late in August 2008. The school year had already started. It was a weekend, and the events started during the daytime and lasted into the night. I remember I was home with all the kids and my husband was at work. My oldest son was alone in his room. Then things started to happen, and I called my in-laws to come to be with me.

While waiting on my in-laws I decided to get the camcorder and set it up on the bookshelf to catch things moving. When I turned it on nothing would happen.

Turned it off and stuff would happen. This demon is very intelligent but stupid because it will be defeated. It keeps throwing the PlayStation games off the shelf and knocks the shelf down. Never could catch that on camera but we saw it. Therefore, I let my son video to try to catch something. Boy did he get something because things got crazy. Stuff was thrown everywhere around the room. We had to duck to keep from being struck in the head.

When my brother-in-law arrived, he stood at my son's bedroom door looking astonished. In the room, things were tossed around and making a big mess. He asked, "What happen?" I told him this demon was mad because we trying to get it to leave. When you demand a demon to leave your home, it will put up a fight to remember.

Matthew 10:1 And when he called unto him his twelve disciples, he gave them power against unclean spirits, to cast them out, and to heal all manner of sickness and all manner of disease.

I asked my son to let me video tape now since the demon showing itself on camera. It now ripped the mini blinds from the window. You could see a reflection of his closet in the window glass. The objects thrown were coming from the closet. I must note that there was a bunk bed on the same side of the closet. It is a small mobile home bedroom no wider than nine feet. The closet door faces to other side of room so you have to be directly in front of the closet to see in it. There is not much room between the closet door and the bunk bed.

While I am video taping him, he was standing in front of the closet and things were flying out over his head toward the bedroom window. To get to the window, the flying items have to go around the bunk bed and turn toward the window. Their path is like an S shape.

He was bravely debunking the demon to leave his closet. Most of you have never faced a demon and told him to go back to hell. That takes guts. The flying items going out had now broken a portion of the bedroom window glass. I did not want all the window glass to be broken, so I raised the window. When I did, the heavy exercise weights flew out followed by other items.

While all this was happening, I had my Bible reading anything in red. I was not a strong Christian person and did not know how to fight this alone. I was reading aloud words of Jesus. I was telling the demon to go back to hell where it came from. I really had no clue on what to say to it. My younger kids thought this was funny. They wanted to see the show, and I did not want see this show. I was scared and in shock over what I was experiencing.

My son was still yelling at the demon to leave his room and our home. As I was watching my son, I was still video taping him. All of a sudden, in the camera lens, I saw my son throw something. At that point, something changed. I told him to stop that he just threw something. I saw it in the camera. He said he did not throw anything. He became upset at my insistence that he threw something. He began to cry at the accusation of something he did not do.

To see, I rewound my tape, and we both reviewed it. It did **not** show him throw anything, just as he said. I told him the devil loves to deceive the eyes, and that is probably what happened. The devil wanted us to argue over what I thought I saw.

When we finished talking, something felt different. We noticed the room was quiet for the first time in many hours. To my delight and surprise, as demanded by my son, it was gone from his room. After inspection, we determined it was also gone from the house!

Luke 9:42 And as he was yet a coming, the devil threw him down, and tare him. And Jesus rebuked the unclean spirit, and healed the child, and delivered him again to his father.

After all this, we had a huge mess to clean up. Everything that was on shelves or the dresser had been thrown on the floor. There were pens, book, CDs, DVD, PlayStation games, pillows, blankets, pictures, and even broken glass. You could not see the floor from all the stuff on it. Even the window blinds were shredded. First time I have seen anything like this ever happen. Seemed like a horror movie in the room.

Later I viewed the video, and it was unbelievable to watch. You can see the stuff coming towards the camera and been thrown. At one point, I saw a black object went pass the camera and disappeared into the closet. It seemed like the demon like being in the closet. As I said earlier in this chapter, the demon had me thinking my son was doing this. However, I know he was not because I saw all this with my own eyes.

After all this was over, we decided to sleep in the devil den. Later that night we actually slept in the living room the center of the home. We dared it to come out and play now. It will no longer but fear in us and we had to show it who was boss of our home. To take authority of your home with paranormal activity you must **never show fear**.

Isaiah 41: 10 Fear thou not; for I am with thee: be not dismayed; for I am thy God: I will strengthen thee; yea, I will help thee; yea, I will uphold thee with the right hand of my righteousness.

Chapter
13
They Return

O n Sunday, August 1, 2010, I was off from work
and home with the kids. As always, being at
home alone with four children they would act out. When
their Dad was at work, I would have a hard time getting
them to mind me. I would get so mad and cry. I could not
get them to act right and did not know why they acted up.
I would get so angry I would yell at them and even spank
them and they would just laugh at me no matter what I
did.

Well, on this one day, because I got so mad and angry
that the demon that haunted me over 2 years ago came
back. By late that evening before my husband got home
from work, I was in the bathroom. I was sitting on the side
of the bathtub for over 30 minutes staring at the wall. I
could not move and froze in that spot.

The kids kept coming in checking on me. I will just
yell at them and tell them to get out of my face. I told
them they needed to stay out of the bathroom because I
knew something was not right. I felt like I did when I had
the demon in me before. That is why I was trying to stay
away from the kids.

When my husband finally came home from work, he walked into the bathroom. He asked, "What is wrong?" I would not even look at him and said nothing is wrong! He told me he had a good day at work. He admitted that he actually preached some to his coworker. When he said the word "preach", I went off on him. I looked at him and cried. He again asked, "What is wrong?"

I then got furious and shaking. He knew then what it was. He knew the very thing we thought we got rid of had returned. The demon had showed itself once again but not for long.

I begin to choke and felt like I would throw up. I felt like I was also having a heart attack. Then my husband walked over to me, laid his hand on my forehead, and said demon I rebuke you in Jesus name! Then after that, the demon left me. I then spoke in tongues for almost 15 minutes. Once all that ended, I felt a calming peace come over me.

Few hours after this all happened I had a Bible two bible verses come to me.

Jeremiah 3:12 Go and proclaim these words toward the north, and say, Return, thou backsliding Israel, saith the Lord; and I will not cause mine anger to fall upon you: for I am merciful, saith the Lord, and I will not keep anger for ever.

Jeremiah3:13 Only acknowledge thine iniquity, thou hast transgressed against the Lord thy God, and hast scattered thy ways to the strangers under every green tree, and ye have not obeyed my voice, saith the Lord.

Throughout the years there have been many more times things would happen. I found a letter I wrote to God asking Him to help me with my anger. Even years after the possession, I still would struggle with being angry all the time. Demons love to stir up conflicts in a home that is trying to live for God and to be happy. They live to come kill, steal and destroy lives of people and families.

I am including a letter I came across that I wrote March 15, 2009 in this chapter to show you how anger still shows itself in a home with demons.

Dear Lord,

Why is it when I try to be a good Christian that the devil always wants to knock me down? I try so hard to stay in your word every day. I watch Christian TV and listen to Christian music. I want so bad to be the best Christian for you Lord. I want so bad to be a good wife and a good mother. I want to be there for my children and not be so angry all the time.

Especially to my oldest son, I treated him terrible and could not stop being this way to him. He did not deserve to be treated that way. I am his mother, not his

enemy. I do love him but why can I not show it to him? I do not want him to hate me! I tell myself each day I will be better to him and I do worse to him. Lord please help me and to show him more love and compassion. I am at the end with this. I do not know where my anger comes from! In Jesus Christ I pray, Amen!

This letter shows you how I was an angry person during this time. I want to add that the anger I had towards my oldest son was not abusive kind of anger. I was a verbal kind of anger towards him. Which today I regret how I treated him. I would yell and scream at him for no reasons I cannot explain. I have harmed none of my children or others during these anger moments. I used many hurtful words, lash out, and say horrible things.

Ephesians 4:29 Let no corrupt communication proceed out of your mouth, but that which are good to the use of edifying, that it may minister grace unto the hearers.

Demons make you do things out of your control but remembering what they make you say is horrible to face. Demons want to control your mind, body and soul. They fed off anger, hate and lies. Demons manipulate your mind into making you feel like you are not doing anything wrong. The dark side of the demons will drag you in and once there, it is hard to get back out of the darkness.

Chapter

14

Child Experiences

I added this chapter to what my children had seen and experienced over the past 11 years. I am writing based on what they tell me of what they can remember. I felt this is an important part of the story because few children have things like this happen in their lifetime. Many people will not believe a lot of this story. However, if this were not true I would have never wasted my time writing this part.

The spiritual things my children have witnessed would scare you enough to make you run out of our home. We have never run from the activity in our home. We all still live in the same home and same bedrooms as normal. When you stop fearing the things that feared us, it will back away and leave you alone. Our children have learned not to be afraid. They are very courageous children for living through all of this. Not much scares them anymore. So now, I will begin by telling you some things they experienced.

I will start one story my daughter experienced of a situation that happened in our master bathroom. She was on her pallet in the living room one day watching TV. She had to go use the bathroom, so she went into ours to use it. When she opened the door, she quickly turned around screaming through the house. I was in the living room and she said, "Mom, there is something in the bathroom staring back at me!" I said, "What is it?" She said," Looks like some white ghostly thing with black hair and eyes staring at me!"

Therefore, I got up out of my chair to go see. As I walked through the house, I spoke in the Holy Spirit. I never saw anything, but I felt a strong presence around the room while walking in. She said it is gone now. I said no, it is not. However, I prayed for it to leave and followed the presence out the front door. I yelled out my front door telling it to leave, never to come back, and never mess with my kids!

2 Corinthians 12:10 Therefore I take pleasure in infirmities, in reproaches, in necessities, in persecutions, in distresses for Christ's sake: for when I am weak, then I am strong.

After this was over, I asked my daughter what exactly she saw. She said, "A white ghostly thing that looked like a young child. It had black eyes and short black hair." The thing was transparent almost invisible but could not see all the way through it. It looked as if it was floating and body was twisted or mangled. Had its head turned little sideways, and it looked creepy she said. It scared her severely.

Times went by after this and I do not recall exact dates or the year's things would happen. I know they would happen as random times for some reason. Like I said, I felt the need to add this into the book. So many things happened over the past 11 years I really wished I wrote them down as they happened. Still until this day, we are experiencing things. I will elaborate on all that at end of this book. Now back to the story.

I recall one thing that happened was when my son found the computer chair moved into the hallway one night. He was going to either go to the bathroom or get water but when he came out, the chair was in the hallway. He came and knocked on our bedroom to tell me the chair was in the hallway. This chair came from our living room. Not sure how it moved, but it was. I put it back and acted as if nothing happened.

Another time is we were all in bed except my two younger sons. They were playing in their room on the PlayStation. My third child, which was another son, had to use the bathroom, and it was after midnight. He went to open the bedroom door and quickly shut it back. He tried calling me on my cell to get me to come in there. Unfortunately, my phone volume was turned down.

My son was too scared to come out, so he sent out his younger brother to come get me. He came and knocked on our bedroom door to wake me up. I opened the door and said," what is wrong?" He said come here I need to show you something. I followed him back toward the hallway leading to the bedroom. Looking down by their bathroom door and saw there was one of our couch pillows on the floor. I asked, "Who put that there?" they said," I do not know!"

I picked up the pillow and placed it back on the couch. I told them to ignore it and go back to bed. We all went back to our rooms and nothing else happened the rest of the night. However, the next night it happened again. This time it moved two couch pillows. So once again, I put them back on the couch and ignored it. Following that, nothing else happened for a long time.

Proverbs 22:6 Train up a child in the way he should go: and when he is old, he will not depart from it.

Until one day, the stove and oven came on by itself. We had a sheet pan sitting on top of two of the burners. The kids smelled something and noticed the stove was smoking. They saw the pan burning and quickly got oven mitts and put it into the sink. They turned off all the burners. We knew then it was back and who did it. Once again, we ignored it.

These demons seem like they want us to fear them not ignore them. Another occurrence took place in the hallway. These demons liked the hallway to play with my sons. One night my third child, the son, was coming down the hallway when he ran into a demon looking thing. He said he saw a pure black demon creature looking at him with red eyes. He said it was crawling on the ground staring at him. Then he said it vanished.

Same son also saw an old white bearded ghostly looking man through the glass of an old family picture frame in the hallway. The ghostly figure was wearing some kind of beanie hat. My son was once again walking down the hallway into the living room and seen him smiling at him. Then the ghost disappeared. He could not make out much more to describe it and not even sure why it appeared. At least it disappeared as fast as it appeared.

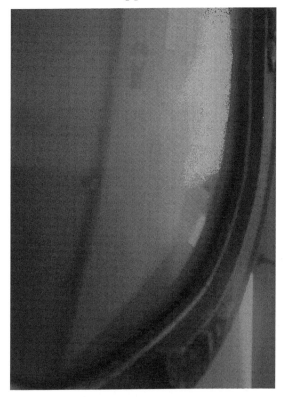

Illustration of Image

I am not sure why my son could see these things more than my other children were. He is the one that can feel the presence of the spirits in the home at times too. My youngest son never had anything he could remember. He was still not born when things started happening. My daughter did not have a lot of activity in her room at all. The spirits never bothered my daughter as they did my son. It seemed like it lived in the boys' room or hallway.

I will never know the reason why all this happened to us. However, it has made a great story to tell. I know this sound like a curse over our home but this may all turned out to be a blessing at the end. If this had never happened, I would have never written a book. Writing is something I never thought I would be doing. I always hated to write with a pen but typing is easier.

I found that in writing it has become my therapy for my mind. Living the life I live is difficult. Nevertheless, no one's life is easy. All my life I have done things the hard way. Writing this book seemed to be an easy way out of my thinking too much over why all this happen to us. I have always heard an over thinker are the best thinkers. Trust me, I am always thinking. I think so much that I may even write a second book but not sure yet what that would be. I will just have to do more think about it.

Chapter

15

The Attacks Continue

Being that demons love coming back to my home, so much I am adding another chapter to this book. Past year we have had random occurrences that would happen. I mentioned some in the previous chapter about my children's experiences. I will now tell you a few more that has happened more recent while I was writing on my last few chapters of this book in past weeks.

One night I came home from work to find a little teddy bear in front of the book shelve in the living room. It was sitting on bottom shelve but was moved in front of bookshelf little ways out. I picked it up and moved it back on the shelf. It was late and everyone was sleep so I waited and asked next morning. When I asked about it, no one knew who moved it.

Few weeks later, there is a small metal picture frame on our TV stand in our bedroom. While walking through to go brush our teeth for the night it flew off the shelf. As we were walking by, I saw it move in the corner of my eye. I looked at my husband like not again. Therefore, I picked it up, put back on the shelf, and ignored it.

The most recent was April 6, 2019, a very rainy stormy day. It was a Saturday evening, and I went to take a bath. When I put my hand in the water, I felt a burning sensation. I look down and saw three scratches on me. After I got out of the tub, I took a photo of the scratches.

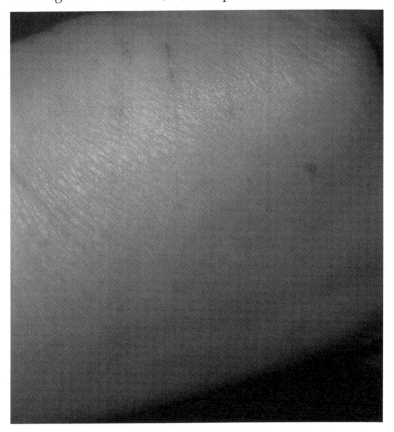

My son took his shower and something had scratched him on his leg.

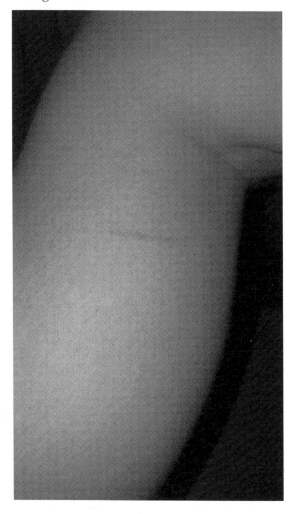

Then, soon my daughter came out of her room and said something scratched her across the stomach.

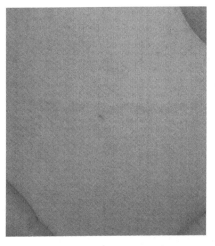

Next day something scratched my son again on his leg.

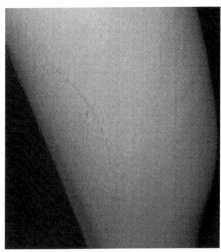

Not sure, why all these scratches kept happening, but it was getting really annoying. My children were becoming scared that something would hurt them. Demons love to put fear in people and they were doing a great job of scaring my kids. As a mom, I knew I had to take charge very soon over all this once again. In addition, I had a plan to do that at the right time.

Once again, two days later before I could begin my plan to get control of my home, the devil tried to take over me. That Monday, April 8, 2019, my husband had just left for work around noon. I was somewhat upset over a small disagreement I had with him that day and was sitting in my chair staring at the walls. My mind was thinking all kinds of crazy thoughts.

Next thing I knew I felt something come over me and could not breathe like it was astounding me. I begin to choke and hold my neck like someone had hands around my neck. I was gasping, choking, and got scared and cried from fear. I was alone and thought something was trying to kill me. I had no marks afterwards. I felt like I got throat punched. This experience was scary for me.

Later the same day, my children came home from school. I did not tell them what happened, yet. When my youngest son walked in the house, he changed into a different child. He became angry, yelled and had a bad attitude. He became uncontrollable. While lying down on the couch he started clapping his hands and kicking his feet. Nothing I said or did would make him stop doing that. He continues to do this for 30 minutes or so. It annoyed me a lot and I was getting frustrated with him.

Once he become himself, he then told me what happened to him and why he acted that way. He said when he walked into the house he felt something gone through his chest and could not breathe. When he felt that, he said was when his mood changed. He said he could not control what he was doing. He felt as something was controlling him at that time. Afterward it looked as if someone had slapped my son across the face. Another example of how these demons can attack.

I need to remind you, this is coming from an 11-year-old, which is same age as what my oldest was when all this started. First paranormal activity we experienced happen April 2008. Therefore, you can say we have been fighting this for 11 years now. Nevertheless, as I said I have a plan, I feel will work this time.

A few weeks ago, I bought sage smudging sticks to help cleanse our home. My Dad sent six crosses he made along with some blessed anointing holy oil. While this was all going on this past week, I was waiting on all this to come in the mail. Once I received all my items, I could now do the cleansing. I actually did the cleansing on April 15, 2019.

I took all six crosses and anointed them with the anointing oil. I then hung them up in rooms and even closets. Then I took the self-blessed anointing oil and anointed all the windows and doors throughout the home. While doing all this I said prayers aloud and everything said in Jesus name. I asked for protection over home and bind up any demonic spirits that may still be in our home.

Once I did all this, I took the sage, burned it, and walked through the whole home. I repeated prayers aloud for all the negative energy and any demonic forces to be gone in Jesus name. Then, asked the Holy Spirit to bring in protection and positive energy in our home.

Proverbs 3:7 Be not wise in thine own eyes: fear the Lord, and depart from evil.

I am up at 2 AM writing this last chapter. Time will tell if the cleansing works. In my opinion, I feel the reason the demons came back to my home is that I have backslide into the ways of the world. At the beginning and throughout this book, I said you have to stay in God's word all times. Without God in your life, the devil will continue to test your faith repeatedly.

So today has been two weeks since I cleansed the house and I can say that we have not had any activity at all. I do not even feel any negative energy like before and can confirm that the cleansing was a success. Now I feel I can close the chapter out and put an ending to this book. I feel confident that the devil has finally been defeated in my home for good.

Please read the last chapter (19) for suggestions to rid your home of unwanted spirits. As best I can tell, it worked. Every room in our home, including closets have blessed crosses hanging. Yes, even in our closets where the evil spirits like to hide. When my Dad was young, he had a battery operated train engine. It was made of stamped metal, 12 inches long. One night, the train engine came out of the closet toward my Dad's bed, turned around and went back into the closet. When he checked the next morning, it had no batteries and he had no explanation of the event. Many people have experiences they cannot explain. If you start to have them, take quick action. It maybe the beginning of the worst days of your life.

Matthew 4: 10 Then saith the Jesus unto him, Get thee hence, Satan: for it is written, "THOU SHALT WORSHIP THE LORD THY GOD, AND HIM ONLY SHALT THOU SERVE.

Matthew 4:11 Then the devil leaveth him, and, behold, angels came and ministered unto him.

Chapter
16
Poems of My Inner Thoughts

Darkness

I lie here in the dark

With those voices in my head

Telling me those lies

And saying I should be dead

I fake a smile on the outside

When I am crying on the inside

I hide the pain well

I feel hopeless and helpless

And I know those are more lies

This darkness is bringing me down

And I feel like I am drowning in my pain

And I have nothing to gain

Secrets

I hide my shame that causes me pain

I have this guilt that I cannot contain

I live with this secret that I now regret

That has put my marriage in a threat

I wished I could go back in time and rewind

This life is not what I planned

But, one day I must rise back up and take a stand

Only I know the secrets that bind me

Now I need to put them all be hide me

Secrets can kill and destroy a soul

So it is time to let them all go

Past

Put the past behind you to forever last
Don't you remember when you were home last?
You said you would stop and come home
But, instead you are always on your phone
You always went out to drink and party
But, don't you know that was not very smarty?
You come home with alcohol on your breath
And also smelling like meth
You are looking like a total mess
And you are always in distressed
Your past will always find you
When you're cold and lonely
And no one is behind you

Be Here

You tell me you love and adore me

But, yet you constantly ignore me

You say you will always be here for me

But, then you go and are free

All I want is for you to be here with me

While you are nowhere to be

You say you will come back to me

But, when I look around you nowhere to be

The games you play with my mind

Is making me want to stay be hide

Let us go back in time

For a new rewind

Drugs

When life is too much for some

They are always on a run

Not knowing where to go

So, they turn to the only one thing they know

Just one hit will pull you in

After that one try will make you high

I do not know why you want to run and hide

All I do is try to love you with all my heart

But, you never know where to start

So, you take another hit to get lit

All you should have done was quit

Now your addicted and cannot stop

You need help I can see

But, you cannot take your eyes off your speed

Anger

When you talk in hate and anger

You make me feel like I am in danger

Why can't you talk to me calmly?

You making me feel lonely

You are talking down to me

When you are in a fit of rage

This is when I feel scared

You should be in a cage

I only want you to love all of me

But, you don't want any part of me

We scream and yell at one another

But, we both don't want any other

Lies

You cheat steal and lie
And I sit here and wonder why
You say I can trust you
But, all I do is bust you
You always seem to hide
But, you know I am not blind
You play tricks with my mind
But you have ran out of time
I do not want you no more
I am now crying on the floor
You walk out of the door
Because you don't want me no more

The Call

You tell me that you love me always

But, you're never with me all days

I wait by my phone for your call

When I hear your ring, I run down the hall

I answer and no one is there

So I sit on the edge of the bed and just stare

Now I am feeling alone and despair

I want to hear your voice

But you give me no choice

I must leave your memory behind

Because I need a mental rewind

Nanny Advice

My grandmother said to stop eating that sugar

And coke

That losing her leg was not even a joke

I did not listen to her in time

Now I sit here not looking so fine

I have all this extra weight

So now, I feel like it is too late

I take this diabetic medicine

While she is already in heaven

She lost her life all too early

When she had her stroke, I was blurry

I do not want to be like her

I know I need to change

So I need help to rearrange

Thoughts

I lay here wide-awake in my bed

With all the thoughts running through my head

I need to get some rest

But, my mind is thinking like for a test

I do not know why I cannot shut my eyes

Do I think I will miss a big surprise?

Oh, how I need some sleep

I do not even want to count sheep

My mind needs a big break

Because I don't want to make a big mistake

I am so tired and weary

Now I do not want anyone near me

God verses Man

God loved us and gave up his only son for us
So why can't we give up our worldly possessions for
Him?
God is full of love and kindness
Man is full of the and greed
God made us
Man kills us
God created us
Man changes us
God forgives
Man hold grudges
God gives
Man takes
God is always with us through hard times
Man leaves us through hard times
God is your friend
Man is your enemy

God is our soul saver

Man is our soul taker

So, who would you want on your side?

God or Man?

Let God

Do not let the devil bring you down
Let God bring you back up
Do not let the devil feed you lies
Let God feed you truth
Do not let the devil pull you into darkness
Let God push you back into the light
Do not let the devil guide you wrong
Let God guide you right
Do not let the devil steal your soul
Let God have your soul
Do not let the devil conform you
Let God transform you
Do not let the devil have victory over your life
Let God bring you into his eternal life
Do not let the devil think he won
Let God show you that He is always on the throne

Pain

I hide behind a fake smile daily

To cover this pain I had lately

You don't know the real me

Only I know the true me

This feeling is killing me inside

I need to run and hide

I feel pain I cannot explain

I have thoughts in my brain

Darkness is over taking me

This pain is always near me

Why can't people hear me?

I cry out for help

But, no one cares

When I am crying

No one knows I am dying

So I am done with trying

Words

Words can cause you pain
Words can make you vain
Words can make you love
Words can make you hate
Words can be said
Words cannot be unsaid
Words can have power
Words can hurt in the midnight hour
Words can break a heart
Words cannot know where to start
Words can bring you down
Words can make you frown
Words can make you angry
Words can make you happy
Words can make you sad
Words can make you mad

Depression

Depression is like being in the dark

Even if you are in the light

Depression is like not being able to breath

Even if you feel like you are drowning inside

Depression is like you are not good enough

Even if you do not feel tough

Depression is like the weight of the world is on you

Even if you feel like no one wants you

Depression makes you feel overwhelmed

Even when you feel like you are being slammed

Depression makes you feel worthless

Even when you feel like this is not worth it

Depression makes you feel hopeless

Even when you have hope

Depression is real

Even when you want to feel

Overcome

When darkness over takes you

Do not let it become what makes you

I have spent years in this mind set

Now I need a divine reset

Do not let your mind wonder

It will go far away over yonder

When in doubt about your life

Think how to overcome all this strife

Your mind can play games with your emotions

When all you trying to do is go through the
motions

Overcoming struggles in life is not easy

But, one day you will see that it is breezy

Friends

Friends are ones that bring you up
They do not need to bring you down
Friends are ones that tell you truth
They do not need to lie behind your back
Friends are ones that are there for you
They do not need to turn on you
Friends are ones that help you
They do not need to step on you
Friends are ones that you can talk to
They do need to ignore you
Friends are the ones that love you
They do not need to hate you

Tired Mind

It is late and I cannot sleep

My mind is running in circles

I am sleepy and tired but mind is awake

I can't stop thinking and I just need a break

I wonder about life and is there more to it

When I try to close my eyes, I think even more

My mind is never at rest

When I am wide-awake I think best

A mind can get lost in the dark with no light

This is why we need God with all our might

Closing my thoughts and mind now

So, you all have a goodnight

My Prayer Poem

Oh, Lord my mind is weary

Things here have been dreary

Thus world is taking your place

It is a disgrace to you

I wait for the day to see your face

How I long for your embrace

I let things come between us

This world has consumed me

Will you condemn me?

Oh Lord my heart is heavy

I can't carry on alone

Please forgive me Oh Lord

Take the world out of me

For Lord I want more of you in me

Life

Life gives you punches you just punch back

Life brings you down just get back up

Life throws stones at you just pick them up and throw them back

Life pushes you just push back

Life tries to defeat you just keep fighting

Life can make you want to give up but do not quit

Life can make you feel wrong just prove it right

Life can judge you but it is not the judge

Life is what you make of it so make the best of what you can do

Life is funny so just humor it

Chapter

17

Photos with Orbs

S ome people may not believe in things that cannot be seen with the naked eye until they can see proof that things can exist. There are things of this world that you cannot explain. I am including photos of orbs that were in our family pictures. I know people will not believe these but these pictures are real as you reading this and seeing them yourself.

I have heard and seen things in past 11 years that people never experience in their lifetime. There is the unknown of the spirit world we cannot see but if you look closely at these pictures, you will find faces in them. Not sure, what they mean or why they showed up, but I would like to think of them has God's angels watching over us.

These are a small sample of our pictures with orbs. They say orb colors have different meanings, so I looked some up to tell you about them.

Example of an orb in the very active kitchen area waiting for me at my bedroom door:

There is a large evil orb by the Christmas tree on upper right. If it was dust or moisture on the lens, why is it BEHIND the tree limb? An image blow up shows it has dark hair on top, two barely visible eyes and half a smile on the right. The other half (left) of the smile is behind the tree branch. The orb is not round but oval like a person's head. This orb picture is one of my unique ones.

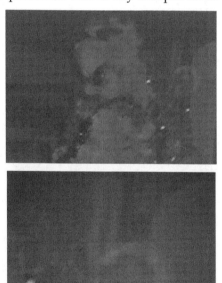

This is a picture of a white orb moving very fast as it leaves my oldest sons chest. It was moving so fast that it left multiple images in a single snap of the shutter.

Are these spirits inside people? The answer is yes. Here is a picture and a sketch of the demon that came out of the head of my daughter at Christmas 2012. How would you like this to be inside your young daughter? Again, it is moving to fast for the human eye to see. Looks like some kind of cartoon character.

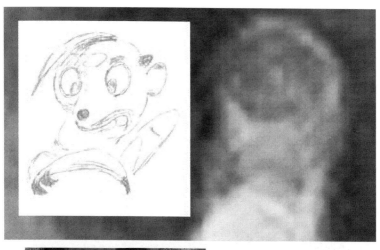

Colored orbs during our Christmas 2008 pictures, as you can see there are many colors and sizes.

12/21/2008

Picture with orbs, 4 years later Christmas 2012.

12/04/2012

More orbs during our 2012 Christmas, as you can see we have had orbs for several years. Most of the orbs were white, so we always figured we had good spirits. We had no other color than these that I showed. They have other meanings to other colors to. As mention before, my Dad had a large (4-inch) bright blue orb in his home. He believes it was his Grandmother, whom he was very close to. She had died the week before he saw it. Blue could mean "Shy, Peaceful, Protection" which makes perfect sense in this case.

The colors of orbs have various meanings that are the accepted norm among some in the paranormal community. We assign the orb colors an emotional attribute instead of a stage of life or some other characteristic driving the determination of color designation. Potential meanings of orb colors:

Black: Malevolent

Blue (dark): Shy spirit

Blue (light): Tranquil, peace

Blue (medium): Protection

Brown: Danger or earthbound

Gold: Angelic, unconditional love

Green: Healing orb or spirit

Lavender: Messenger from God

Orange: Protection, forgiveness

Peach: Spirit sent to comfort you

Pink: Accepting spirit

Purple: Orb of information

Red: Anger or passion

Silver: Messenger

Violet: Guide for spiritual matters

White: Protection of holy light and power

Yellow: Warning

Some researchers theorize that if an orb is that of a deceased person, then the color is controlled by the aura of the person's soul in a disembodied form. Other paranormal and supernatural investigators say the angelic energy creates gold and purple orbs.

We describe chakra orbs as energy emitted by a person's own chakra system, and spirit chakras that take on the colors of the spirit's chakras. *"Chakras are energy centers. Although most people have heard of seven chakras, there are actually 114 in the body. The human body is a complex energy form; in addition to the 114 chakras, it also has 72,000 "nadis," or energy channels, along which vital energy, or "prana," moves. When the nadis meet at different points in the body, they form a triangle. We call this triangle a chakra, which means "wheel." We call it a wheel because it symbolizes growth, dynamism and movement, so even though it is actually a triangle, we call it a chakra. Some of these centers are very powerful, while others are not as powerful. At different levels, these energy centers produce different qualities in a human being."* (The 7 Chakras and Their Significance to Your Life, BySadhguru, Contributor-Mystic, Yogi and Founder, Isha Foundation)

There are reports orbs have shown up within a person's aura in Kirlian and regular photographs. It is believed the orbs are the spirits of loved ones attracted to the person. *"Kirlian photography is a collection of photographic techniques used to capture the phenomenon of electrical <u>coronal discharges</u>. It is named after <u>Semyon Kirlian</u>, who, in 1939, accidentally discovered that if an object on a <u>photographic plate</u> is connected to a high-voltage source, an image is produced on the photographic plate. Paranormal claims have been made about Kirlian photography, but these claims are unsupported by the scientific community."* (https://en.wikipedia.org/wiki/Kirlian_photography)

If the orb is paranormal, the color of the orb may relate to energy. There are multiple theories about what orb colors mean, with many colors potentially meaning many things. (Many possibilities) In most cases, people suggesting orb colors and assigning meanings do so based on their spiritual beliefs. It is important to note these are only spiritual theories and have no true basis in scientific fact.

One theory of orb colors is the orbs are simply manifesting in the best way they can. In these cases, the colors may have no meaning at all. But, the spirit could be trying to communicate something with their color.

Clear orbs may be an attempt to communicate with you. The spirit may try to let the living know that a significant event happened in that location and the spirit wants help to move on.

Spiritually, **white or silver** might mean the spirit connects with a higher source. Some believe orbs that are either white or silver are a sign that the spirit is trapped on this spiritual plane. They perceive white energy to be highly positive in nature.

Spiritually, many feel **black or brown** colors are associated with bad spiritual vibrations. Some people interpret this as evil although maybe not. When black or brown orbs appear, some interpret them as the area may be unsafe. Examine the area, and if you feel uncomfortable or unsafe, leave.

They associate **red and orange** colors with safety, security, or a sense of belonging. They are often associated with strong emotions, anger and passion, but this may not be the case for ghost orbs. Some paranormal investigators believe a red or orange orb is a protector. This could be someone who will keep watch or act as a caretaker.

Green is associated with the heart and nature. Green orbs could indicate the presence of a human spirit as opposed to one that was never on Earth as a human. They may also represent love or oneness with nature.

Blue is associated with psychic energy and the truth. It is a calming color, and some associate it with spiritual guidance. Blue orbs can be a sign of a calming energy while others feel they indicate the presence of a spirit guide.

Gray or smoky orbs may show depression, fear or ambivalence. Smoky color, like the color gray, may indicate confusion or trouble.

Pink orbs are messengers of love, hope, encouragement, or peace. This can be universal love, such as from a guide, teacher or archangel. It can be the love of a deceased family member who is saying they are still with you.

Some camera lenses have coatings with different colors in them. Sometimes these colors show in orbs that are photographic artifacts and has nothing to do with the paranormal. This is also known as a lens flare orb. Orbs are very common in paranormal photography.

Items can cause orbs to appear including reflective surfaces, dust, rain, water spots, and bugs. Therefore, many investigators do not consider orbs as paranormal evidence because there are too many natural world explanations. It is still possible that some orbs can be paranormal.

People believe they see faces or angels in orbs, but this is most likely a trick of the mind called pareidolia. *"Definition of pareidolia. : the tendency to perceive a specific, often meaningful image in a random or ambiguous visual pattern The scientific explanation for some people is **pareidolia**,* *or the human ability to see shapes or make pictures out of randomness. Think of the Rorschach inkblot test."* (Merriam-Webster)

Are orbs good or bad? They may be photographic lens issues or something more. While many researchers have compiled data on ghost orbs and colors, no one can be certain about meanings. Most people associate wispy apparitions with the term "ghost", but some think orbs are a ghost. That is debatable. An orb does not necessarily signify that a ghostly spirit is nearby. A true ghost orb is spiritual. Some people believe when they see an orb, they are actually viewing a deceased person's soul. Others believe spheres are actually hosts to many spirits, all contained within the orb. Others believe these orbs are just spirits that they were never a human body. Some believe they are evidence of the spiritual side of nature. Some ghost psychics say the earth can manifest into a spirt that has never been human and is evil.

How can you identify an orb as a ghost? There is no answer. Some believe an orb is the form a spirit takes as it moves about. There are various reasons why a circle. It can enclose the spirit, contain more than one, easy to travel and is a natural shape that represents eternity. Many people base their beliefs that they have encountered a ghost when they see an orb in a photo. Unfortunately, these orbs mostly are not a ghost. I have taken many pictures with non-ghost orbs but some that are clearly inhibited.

Chapter

18

Orb's Matrix Illustrations

These illustrations are for sale on eBay. The proceeds generated from the sales of the "Orb Matrix" illustrations will be used for my children's education. I hope you see in your heart to help give them what I did not have.

Heather Alfred

The following illustrations were conceived from images derived from blow-up orb images taken by Heather. The orbs used were different from a common round colored orb. Each has its own personality. The orb size was increased and lines drawn around the "objects" inside the orb. The orb lined drawing was visually interpreted and transferred to a poster board. The poster board was colorized using ink or chalk or both. Photos were taken of the sketch with text and orb images added to make a poster. A lot of work went into these and we hope you will purchase them. We were able to locate a printer that had a reasonable cost. They are truly one of a kind directly from the supernatural! Search eBay for "Orb Matrix".

Here are some of my favorite orbs followed by the orb matrix illustrations sold on eBay:

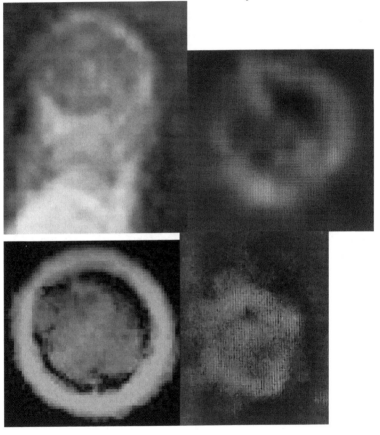

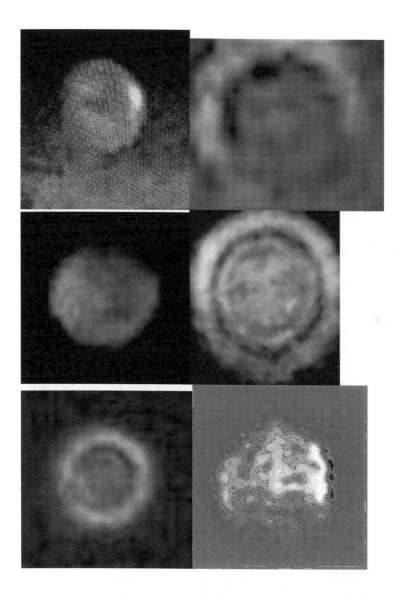

Orb Matrix Illustration 01

Was seen lurking above the Christmas tree watching us open gifts.

Orb Matrix Illustration 02

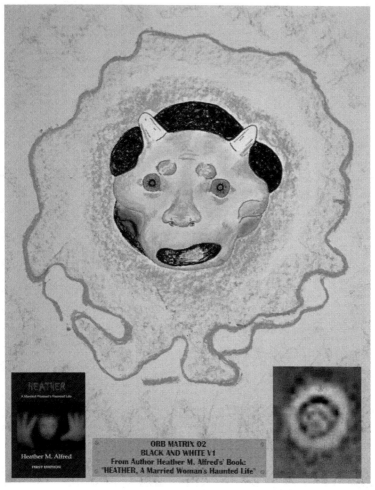

Another version of the same orb.

Orb Matrix Illustration 03

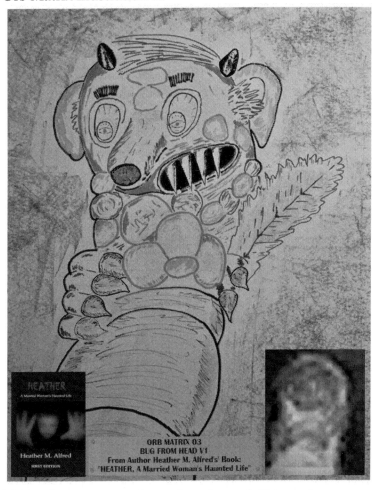

This orb came out of my daughters left temple.

Orb Matrix Illustration 04

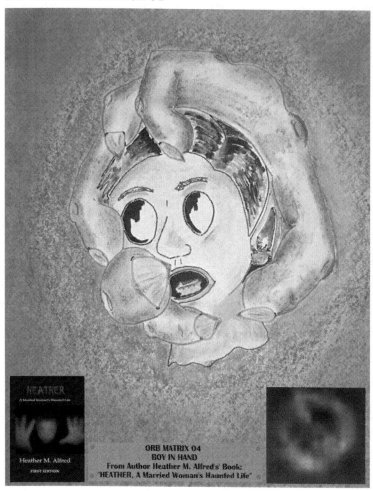

This orb presented itself during Xmas 2008

Orb Matrix Illustration 05

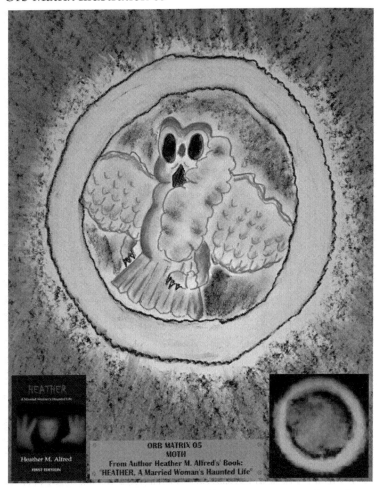

This orb appears to be a cross between an owl and a moth. It seems to have something it is chasing that looks like a fly egg almost in its grasp.

Orb Matrix Illustration 06

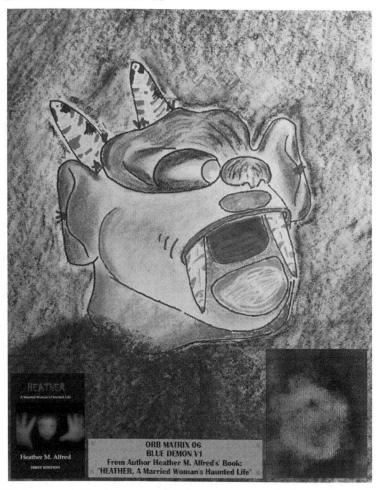

This is one image you get from an orb when filtered.
Another version is also included in this chapter.

Orb Matrix Illustration 07

ORB MATRIX 07
ANGEL IN HAIR
From Author Heather M. Alfred's' Book:
"HEATHER, A Married Woman's Haunted Life"

I told the illustrator that I see an angel in my daughter's hair. He agreed and did an illustration to help you see it.

Orb Matrix Illustration 08

ORB MATRIX 08
THREE HEADS
From Author Heather M. Alfred's Book:
"HEATHER, A Married Woman's Haunted Life"

Orb Matrix Illustration 09

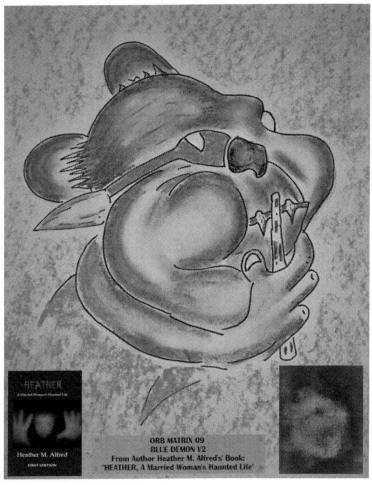

As you can see when you apply filters, the one interpreting the image may see more than one possibility.

Orb Matrix Illustration 10

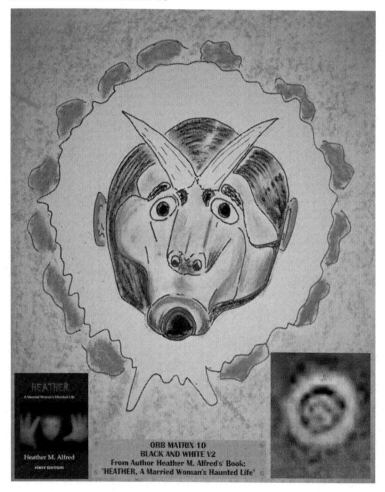

ORB MATRIX 10
BLACK AND WHITE V2
From Author Heather M. Alfred's' Book:
"HEATHER, A Married Woman's Haunted Life"

Orb Matrix Illustration 11

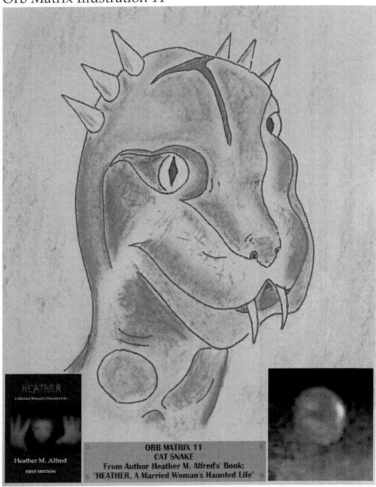

ORB MATRIX 11
CAT SNAKE
From Author Heather M. Alfred's Book:
"HEATHER, A Married Woman's Haunted Life"

We made a movie of this one and put it on YouTube.

Orb Matrix Illustration 12

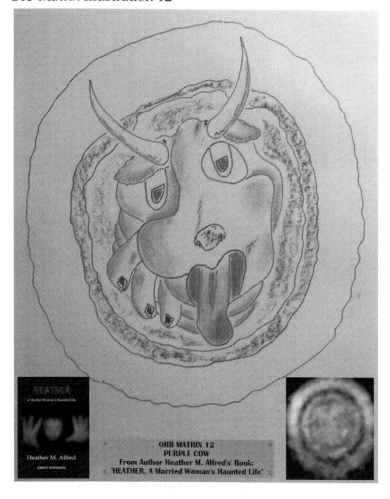

Orb Matrix Illustration 13

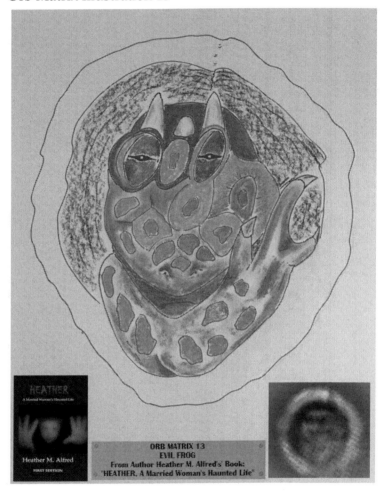

ORB MATRIX 13
EVIL FROG
From Author Heather M. Alfred's Book:
"HEATHER, A Married Woman's Haunted Life"

Orb Matrix Illustration 14

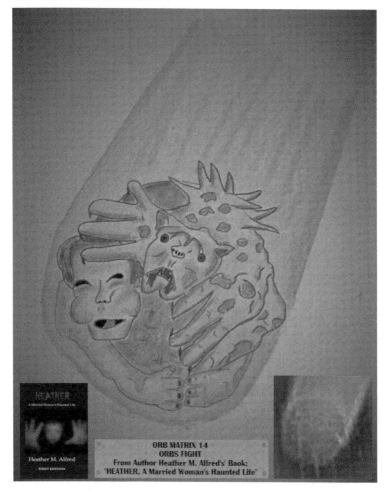

Orb Matrix Illustration 15

Orb Matrix Illustration 16

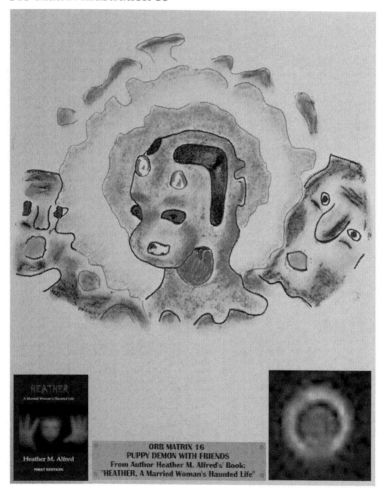

Orb Matrix Illustration 17

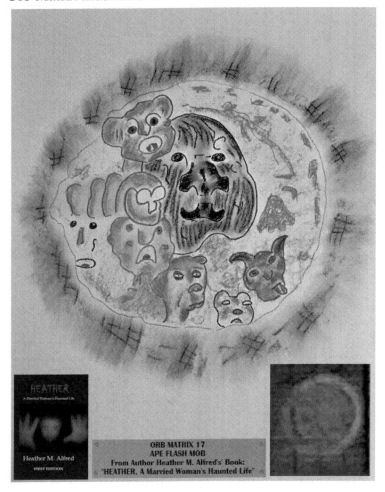

Orb Matrix Illustration 18

ORB MATRIX #18
MAN CHANGING INTO DEMON
From Author Heather M. Alfred's Book:
"HEATHER, A Married Woman's Haunted Life"

Orb Matrix Illustration 19

Orb Matrix Illustration 20

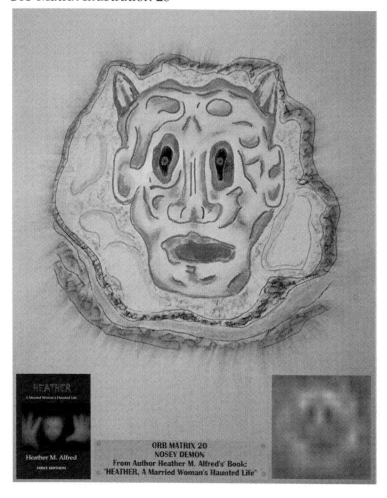

ORB MATRIX 20
NOSEY DEMON
From Author Heather M. Alfred's' Book:
"HEATHER, A Married Woman's Haunted Life"

Orb Matrix Illustration 21

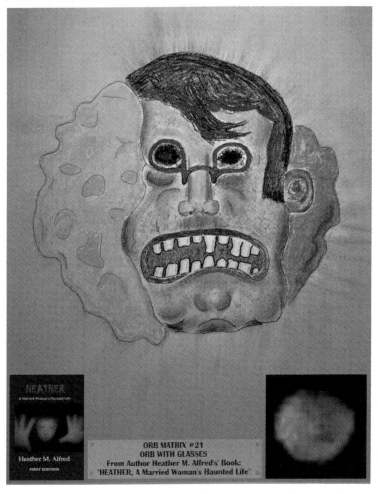

This one was photographed flying around outside our home on the "Blood Moon" night of 2019.

Orb Matrix Illustration 22

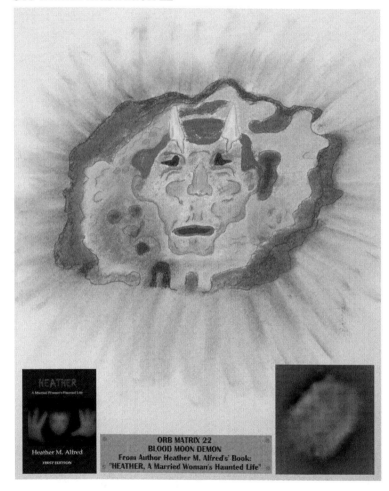

Orb Matrix Illustration 23

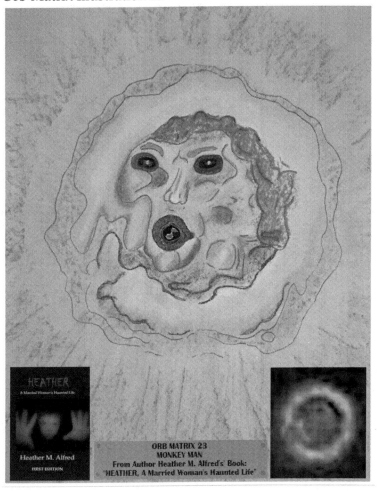

ORB MATRIX 23
MONKEY MAN
From Author Heather M. Alfred's Book:
"HEATHER, A Married Woman's Haunted Life"

Chapter
19
Closing Remarks & References

I would like to thank my Dad for giving me the encouragement to write this book. He was a big help in making this all come together and I could not done this without him. His motivation to push me to finish is what I needed. My Dad has always been an inspiration in my life and I give him a lot of the credit for this book. He took part in putting it all in order and was my advisor and editor to this book. Dad you pushed me to finish something for once in my life and I thank you for it.

I also want to thank my family for giving me the time I needed to write. It is hard to work a full time job and take care of a house, kids, and husband while writing a book. It has taken over 11 years to get to this point of telling our story. This book took a year to write and I will remember this for rest of my life. I am thankful I have a family that can stand with me through all the times we had to fight for our home.

I hope and pray this book will help someone fight the battles of the devil. These little demons are always on the prowl looking for their next victim. You need to beware of the schemes they play and do not let them take over your home. Once in your home they are hard to remove if you keep opening that door.

I have shared with you on how to get rid of these demons and how to protect yourself from them. You must stay in God's word and I say that with emphasis. God is the only way to help win a battle over the devil. I cannot stress this enough and is the reason I keep repeating. If you are not a believer of God then you may lose a fight with the devil.

Backsliding can cause a vicious cycle and never ending fight. Trust me; I learned the hard way and still learning to this day. Life is already hard enough. If you become conformed to the world then the world will suck the life out of you. The devil lives in this world and he is always waiting for the right moment to attack us. I speak from experience. This is why I wrote this book.

In order to help those that want to protect your home, there are things you can do yourself. Get a black cross. Before hanging it on the wall, you should bless it. Here are some suggestions I found to help you prepare your home:

Do this before any unwanted supernatural activity begins. You can place various objects, such as crosses around your home to act as a symbolic sign to the Spirit World that they need to stay out. If you have watched any of the television shows about the supernatural, you know you do not want that happening in your home nor to your loved ones. If you are having supernatural problems in your home, it is suggested by some to place black crosses in each room including closets (See Number 6 of the "12 Ways to Protect Your Family from Evil" list below). You absolutely need black (Blessed) crosses in your children's rooms. Many times spirit portals are located in a closet because there is no hanging cross in it. They are also known to be in children's rooms because they are more sensitive to spirits. Do not take a chance. Beautiful stained wooden crosses are nice but black has a special meaning:

This loving and sorrowful contemplation was the core of his spirituality and the means by which the Congregation was to accomplish its mission. In the Rule for the Poor of Jesus, Paul had written: *"Dearly beloved, you must know that the main object in wearing black (according to the special inspiration that God gave me) is to be clothed in mourning for the Passion and Death of Jesus. For this purpose let us never forget to have always with us a constant and sorrowful remembrance of Him. And so let each of the Poor of Jesus take care to instill in others meditation on the suffering of our Jesus."* - Diary of St Paul of the Cross, Nov 26, 1720

Get any size black cross for each room, bless it and hang it up. You can have crosses blessed or you can bless them. A cross loses its blessing if it is sold for a profit, or if it is substantially broken. Therefore, we cannot bless or have it blessed for you. An un-ordained person is welcome to conduct blessings, but these are pleas to God, not the ordained creation of a sacramental object. There are no guarantees that the cross will become holy, or consecrated. It may not be suitable for use in church ceremonies until it has received an official blessing by a church leader. Blessing the cross yourself may not carry the same effect as a priest's blessing, but anyone may plea to God to bless his or her cross or other object. You may recite any prayer while doing so, for instance one of the following:

Lord, bless this Cross that it may be an instrument of Your Divine Mercy in the Name of the Father, and of the Son, and of the Holy Spirit, Amen.

Bless this Cross in the Name of the Father, and of the Son and of the Holy Spirit, Amen.

Here are 12 ways you can take to protect your family from evil spirits if you are feeling spiritually attacked courtesy of the Catholic Church internet site:

1. St. Michael Prayer and Chaplet – In addition to praying the St. Michael prayer, there is also a St. Michael chaplet that you can pray with a special set of beads or on the free Laudate app for smartphones. You can also ask a priest to pray the St. Michael prayer over you or your family.

2. Guardian Angels – For parents who feel their children are undergoing spiritual warfare, you can ask your guardian angel to work with their guardian angel to protect them.

3. Fasting – Fasting combined with prayer, as said in the Bible and by many saints, is one of the most effective ways to ensure your prayers are heard.

4. Blessed Salt – Have a priest, deacon or exorcist bless a container of salt. In addition to cooking with it, sprinkle it around your house as a shield.

5. Bless Your Home – Have a priest bless your home at least yearly.

6. Crucifix – Have a crucifix in every room of your home, especially your children's rooms and by the front door.

7. Rosary – Pray it daily, as a family — even a decade — if you can!

8. Blessings – Bless your children with the sign of the cross with holy water (you can get it at the baptismal in your church) before bed and before they leave the house.

9. Backpacks – For kids, place a blessed rosary and Miraculous Medal in their backpack, so it will always be close to them. You can also use a St. Benedict medal with an exorcism blessing.

10. Adoration – Spend time in adoration or in front of the Blessed Sacrament.

11. Miraculous Medal – Place a Miraculous Medal underneath the mattress of every person in your house.

12. Prayer – Suggested Prayers

"Heavenly Father, if there are demons prowling around looking for the souls of my family, I ask in the name of your son, Jesus Christ, that you cast them out and protect us from the evil one. Amen."

Ask the blood of Jesus to cover the person and protect them. It was the blood that Christ shed that washed away evil.

With the cross of Jesus I come against and I pull down all demonic strongholds in PERSON'S NAME's mind and body in the name of the father and the son and the Holy Spirit.

With the cross of Jesus I come against and I break all demonic strongholds in PERSON'S NAME's mind and body in the name of the father and the son and the Holy Spirit.

With the cross of Jesus I come against and I demolish all demonic strongholds in PERSON'S NAME's mind and body in the name of the father and the son and the Holy Spirit.

I seal PERSON'S NAME's mind and body with the blood of Jesus and reclaim all of its territories for Christ in the name of the father and the son and the Holy Spirit

I asked The blessed Virgin Mary to bind and cast out all demonic influences from PERSON'S NAME bringing them to the foot of the cross of her son Jesus where they are defeated forever never to return. AMEN

Note: All my Bible verses came from the King James Version Bible

https://www.gotquestions.org/do-_demons-exist.html

https://paranormal.lovetoknow.com/Ghost_Orbs_Different_Colors

https://www.thoughtco.com

The 7 Chakras and Their Significance to Your Life, BySadhguru, Contributor-Mystic, Yogi and Founder, Isha Foundation

https://en.wikipedia.org/wiki/Kirlian_photography

http://www.catholicnewbie.com/tag/prayers-to-defend-against-evil/

Diary of St Paul of the Cross, Nov 26, 1720

Made in the USA
Columbia, SC
16 May 2019